AN INVITAT

DARTMOOR

and

Its surrounding Towns & Villages

A comprehensive guide to Dartmoor, its folklore, its history and its people.

Places to visit,
Inns, Pubs, Hotels and Restaurants

By

JOY DAVID

THE PERFECT COMPANION
FOR LOCALS & VISITORS

The Writer, Joy David, wishes to thank Mervyn Woodward, Hilary Kent and Catherine Mitchell for their enthusiasm and dedication in the compilation of this book. A personal acknowledgment as well to John Weir of the Dartmoor National Park Authority whose help and advice has been much appreciated.

Thanks are also given to Emma Macleod-Johnstone, and Andrew Forsyth for all the drawings.

Acknowledgements

ISBN 1 899311 00 9
First published in 1994

Published by Invitation Press Limited, Fleet House, 15, Trafalgar Street, Plymouth, PL4 9PE. Telephone: (0752) 256013 Fax: (0752) 250503

Typeset by
Typestyle (The P.C.Bureau) Devon Tel: (0752) 698668
Printed & bound in Great Britain by
The Book Factory

CONTENTS

Includes

AN INVITATION TO

DARTMOOR

and

Its surrounding Towns & Villages

INTRODUCTION

I have been fortunate enough to visit, at one time or another, every National Park in Britain. Each has its own charm from the loneliness of Northumberland to the gentle charm of the New Forest which has recently come under the banner of National Parks but for me nothing will ever compare with the wild, rugged beauty of Dartmoor with its hidden villages, its ancient stones, rushing waterfalls and most importantly the people who have made this place of enchantment their home. Many would live nowhere else. For the visitor like myself there is much to learn if one is to appreciate the true beauty - and danger - of the moor. There are rules to obey; disobedience can result in disaster. Make sure before you start any excursion that you have stout walking shoes and a good map. Dartmoor is without peer in its beauty but it is as well to heed the rules.

My purpose in writing this book was to indulge my love of Dartmoor and take the opportunity to share with the reader some of my favourite places, hotels and pubs as well as the delightful villages and the small, busy towns like Tavistock, Okehampton, Bovey Tracey and Ashburton which stand at the entrance to the moor. I discovered excellent pubs, enjoyed a night or two in pretty hotels and guest houses and found myself fed on some of the best West Country fare. In addition I found it to be a remarkable aid in my battle against cancer - there is something so permanent about Dartmoor which nothing can destroy.

I hope this gently, meandering book will help you to understand and love Dartmoor as much as those who live there, and will give you as much pleasure as I have found in writing it.

How lucky we Devonians are to have the magic, the mystery, the awe, the splendour and the beauty of DARTMOOR NATIONAL PARK on our doorsteps, for this is the case whether you live north, south, east or west. From my home city of PLYMOUTH I can be on the edge of the moor within ten minutes or so. It is a different world and one to be explored, loved and cherished but always remembering that it is not a place in which to take chances. The weather can change in minutes from glorious sunshine to impenetrable mists. On a summer's day it is the most welcoming of places and it is difficult to imagine that it is untrustworthy. It is easy to get lost and very frightening. In heavy rain it becomes positively sinister. This is why there are fundamental lessons to learn about Dartmoor before you start exploring. Make sure for starters that you have sturdy shoes, a map and compass. Winter walking equipment should also include waterproof gaiters, a tough cagoule, waxed, waterproof mittens which can be worn comfortably over woollen gloves. You might think it far fetched to carry a 'bivvy sack' - a strong plastic bag big enough to get inside if you should have an accident but it could save your life. First aid equipment, a whistle and a torch all have their uses. Steady flashes in the dark from a torch will help to alert search parties. Six blasts from a whistle every minute for a regular period could well be heard by rescuers. If you are lost in fog always follow a stream - every one on the moor eventually leads to a road or a house. It is good to wear bright colours as well which are more easily spotted. It is a National Park, but that does not mean you have unlimited access. For example, it is an offence to drive a car more than 15 yards off the road.

The Dartmoor ponies run wild and there is no more beautiful sight than these sturdy creatures. They are nosy and friendly but you are asked not to feed them. The reason is simple; it encourages them to stray onto the roads, putting themselves and road users into danger. There is a severe fine for those who do not heed this request. Another important point is to take notice if red flags are flying on the north side of the moor. This means that military training is taking place. Disobey the warning and you could get shot!

You are asked not to play golf on the Dartmoor commons. It may endanger other people, stock or wildlife and it can be an offence under the byelaws. For those who want to enjoy a round of golf there are many courses around the moor which are listed at the back of this book.

Also under the Dartmoor National Park byelaws the flying of Model Aircraft requires prior consent of the landowner and the National Park Authority. It is also an offence to land or take off on any of the Dartmoor commons without proper consent so Hang Gliding is out unless permission has been sought. The South Devon Hang Gliding Club run by Rupert Lane at Higher Uppacott, Poundsgate, Telephone number 03643 243 are the people to consult.

Another sport that is limited because of potential disturbance to winter spawning and summer game fishing is Canoeing. However, access arrangements have been made on certain stretches of the River Dart from October 1st until the end of February only. Details of this facility are available from Mountain Stream Activities whose excellent establishment I have written about later in the chapter.

Dartmoor is wonderful for walking dogs but you are asked to keep your pet under close control and prevent it from chasing sheep or other stock. From March to June, please keep dogs on leads to avoid disturbance to ewes, lambs and ground-nesting birds.

Another simple request, if you are bringing your horse onto the moor, is that you ride with consideration for others and avoid galloping when the going is soft. The shod hoof can cause considerable damage to fragile soils. As for Rock Climbing there is no restriction where there is right of access but when the rocks lie on private land permission to climb must be sought from the landowner. At the back I have listed a number of books which are very helpful and includes ROCK CLIMBS IN THE SOUTH WEST, SOUTH DEVON AND DARTMOOR, by Pat Littlejohn and Pete O'Sullivan.

A guide for cyclists wanting to use Dartmoor is available from all National Park Information Centres but there are a few important points to remember. You should not cycle on public footpaths, common land or open moorland. Cycling is only allowed on public roads, byways open to all traffic, public bridlepaths and Forestry Commission roads.

What is unchanging about Dartmoor is the love affair that people have with it. It is almost like a good marriage; it is sometimes turbulent, sometimes inexplicable, mysterious, infuriating, but always beloved. Within its encompassing arms you wake in the morning never knowing what the day will bring. People who live on the moor are a breed of their own, generous enough to want to share their love affair with outsiders and astonished if your reaction is not the same as theirs. No intrusion of man, since prehistoric times, has managed to conquer the wildness of this granite mass, some 130,000 acres in all.

Perhaps a short history of Dartmoor would be applicable here but the main purpose of this book is to help you enjoy all that the area has to offer both on the moor and in the surrounding towns and villages. There is so much to see and do.

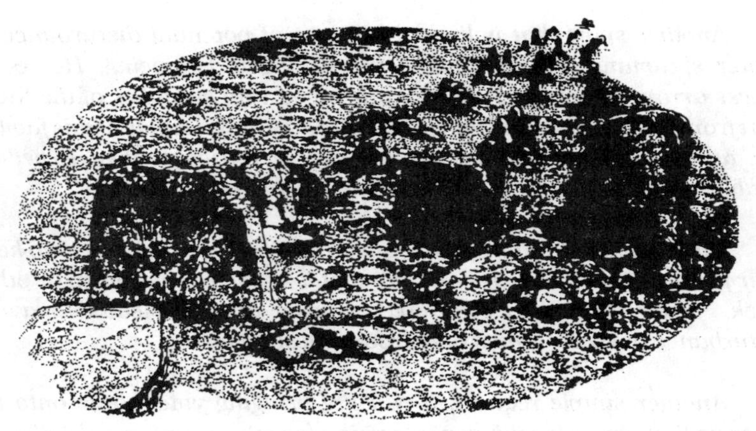

Dartmoor

I had always thought that during the British Ice Age Dartmoor was covered in ice, but this is not so, which is why it is more than likely that Old Stone Age Man hunted here around about 15,000BC. You will find no written evidence of this but it is generally accepted as highly probable. The first evidence of human occupation came from the discovery of flint tools at various places such as POSTBRIDGE, GIDLEIGH COMMON and EAST WEEK. They would have been in use in temporary camps of the Middle Stone Age man from 15,000BC to 3,500BC.

These were nomadic people who lived from the skill of their hunters as well as gathering fruits and edible roots to give them a varied diet. From 3,500 to 2,000BC the more advanced New Stone Age man made much better tools, used pottery and clothed themselves in woven articles, and had even settled sufficiently to cultivate cereal crops. Many places in Dartmoor have yielded up examples of their flint arrowheads but no pottery or dwellings have ever been found. The hunters, in order to drive game, had begun clearing parts of Dartmoor by burning the forest and this went on right through the Neolithic period and carried on into the Bronze Age. It is the Bronze Age from 2,000BC to 500 BC which has yielded up great riches.

There are more Bronze Age remains on Dartmoor than in any other comparable part of England. The remains of Bronze Age homes are to be seen in the many hut circles; some of the finest examples are at GRIMSPOUND. I wondered where the name 'Beaker Folk' came from, and I learnt that early Bronze Age people became known by this nickname because of the distinctive type of pottery which has been found in their graves. One might have supposed that there would be metal artefacts but the acid soil of Dartmoor destroys not only metal objects but human remains as well. No wonder so many murder stories have been based on the moor - the evidence would simply be destroyed by the soil.

As well as the hut circles, there are many stone circles, stone rows and single standing stones known as Menhirs to be found all over Dartmoor. Many of them are part of burial chambers such as the stone row at DOWN TOR, but most remain a mystery just waiting to be solved, although there are no lack of suggestions as to what they might be. Without a written record anywhere these Bronze Age folk have told us much about themselves from the remains on Dartmoor. We know they were pastoral people, who kept animals and built their homes in pounds or vast enclosures to keep their livestock safe from the wild animals which roamed the moor - there are tales of wild animals still roaming the moor!

If we had to live in the type of huts they constructed for themselves we would probably die of hypothermia but they were snug and fortunately lived on a Dartmoor which was considerably warmer than it is now. These huts were built with a couple of stone circles about four feet high. The space between the two circles was filled with earth which acted as a sort of insulation. Inside the ground was excavated to a depth of about three feet and bang in the middle they erected a pole which held the roof of branches covered with turves. No beds of course, but a sleeping platform built of stones. Generally speaking they cooked on fires outside the homes but presumably to combat bad weather they had an indoor cooking fire whose smoke was channelled to escape through a hole in the roof.

The world famous archaelogist Lady Fox was responsible for our knowledge of the Iron Age men of Dartmoor. Her excavations at KES TOR in 1951 and 1952 unearthed an iron smelter's house and workshop as well as a number of other houses making up an Iron Age settlement. Iron

Age Hill forts remain to remind us of this important time. There are three around FINGLE GORGE which is where you will also find the romantic and beautiful FINGLE BRIDGE hidden away at the end of a long, winding, leafy lane that seems to descend forever from the unspoiled village of DREWSTEIGNTON with its thatched cottages and medieval hilltop church as well as the totally unaltered old village hostelry, THE DREW ARMS. Of the three forts, PRESTONBURY can be clearly seen from the bridge, WOOSTON is down river and when you see it on a spring morning with the sun behind you - a breathtaking sight. The third is CRANBROOK near Moretonhampstead.

Fingle Bridge is worth seeing in its own right. It is a pack-horse bridge and dates back to Elizabethan times, if not earlier, straddling a river which dances and cavorts as it runs in and out and over the many boulders strewn in its path. The bridge always conjures up a picture of Roundheads and Cavaliers in my imagination, for once you cross the bridge there are only paths which were probably the way the merchants came with their laden pack horses. It was ideal territory for skirmishes between the warring factions. The sound of clashing swords beneath the trees and then the sound of horses hooves as they carried the victors away into safety leaving the vanquished behind to seek sanctuary or help from local people - if any were to be found. If you wander up into the woods you will find the little grave of a Cavalier bringing a touch of reality into what happened so very long ago..

The Price family own and run THE ANGLERS REST at Fingle Bridge, as they have done for generations. It all started in 1837 when Jessie Ashplant set up a little stall in the open air to provide food for fishermen. She walked down from Drewsteignton every day and stayed

Fingle Bridge

until dusk. Eventually she persuaded her husband to build her a lean-to shed which at least kept the elements at bay! Now it is an attractive licensed restaurant where you will be well fed, and on warm days find enjoyment sitting outside watching the waters run down stream. At one time you would have seen some small businesses across the bridge, charcoal, tannery and a mill. They have all gone and now all that is left is the sheer beauty of the river, the packhorse bridge and the trees.

Just a stone's throw from sleepy Drewsteignton is CASTLE DROGO, owned by the National Trust. It acquired its name from the Drogo who owned the manor in the days of Richard the Lionheart. It is an amazing place and has the honour of being the last castle to be built in this country. Julius Drewe was responsible for it, and he was the man who made a fortune by buying tea in China and selling it through his chain of shops, the Home and Colonial Stores.

He wanted the very best and it was to Sir Edward Lutyens that he went, demanding of that fine architect something totally unusual. Building was started in 1910 on a promontory which stands at least 1,000 feet above sea level and commands some of the finest views in the whole of Devon.

Lutyens plans were too ambitious. Julius Drewe had allowed £60,000 for the building and the gardens. It does not sound much today but, for something around the two hundred pound mark, you could buy a four bedroomed terraced house at that time, which puts it into perspective.

What was built was a third of the size intended but it is still huge and Lutyens has managed to capture a sense of medieval times, even without the great hall and the other rooms that his original plans demanded. The windows with their small panes are distinctly in the manner of Tudor times.

There are many grand and stately chambers; splendid tapestries line the walls of the main staircase. The magnificent drawing room has views of Dartmoor from three sides, and in the kitchen there is a table which will intrigue every housewife. It is round, made of solid beech and even the pastry boards have been curved to fit.

Drogo Castle has a feeling of home about it inspite of its size. Sadly, Julius Drewe lived only a year after it was finished but at least he had achieved his dream; a castle built in the medieval style complete with a chapel.

The gardens are lovely and you can even play croquet on the lawn if you wish. It is open from Good Friday until the end of October daily 11-6. You can get coffees, light lunches and teas at the castle and there is reasonable access to the house and most of the garden for anyone in a wheelchair.

I took a slight diversion there, but that is one of the great joys of Dartmoor; there are always things you want to see and explore which will take you along divergent ways.

It is odd that Dartmoor did not appear in the Domesday Book but some 40 manors whose lands lie in the Moor are mentioned. You will find them mainly on the eastern and north-eastern slopes. Some are still occupied and appear to remain much as they were in the time of the Domesday Book. HOUND TOR MEDIEVAL VILLAGE is the most written about and best documented of these sites. Beneath the ruins the remains of earlier wattle and turf houses have been discovered.

Manaton is overlooked by the lofty MANATON ROCKS, which if seen in autumn aglow with the berries of holly and mountain ash, will remind you that there are not many more shopping days to Christmas. Sit awhile close to the Tor and it is a pound to a penny you will hear the keening of buzzards, a sound regularly heard on the moor.

From Manaton you are within spitting distance of one of my favourite places, BECKY FALLS. It is high up in the solitude of Dartmoor and you approach it through glorious woods. On one side of the road there is a car park, where, if you have any sense, you will don stout shoes or wellies, before making the descent to Becka Brook. Here the water cascades over and between massive boulders, until with a roar it reaches its peak and falls, in sparkling torrents, on its way to the sea. This enchanted world is at its best after the mid-winter rains. I last saw it on a sunlit November morning when the autumn colours of the leaves and bushes added lustre to the silver grey of the tumbling water.

Becky Falls is a natural playground for children and the abundant flora,fauna and wildlife make it even more special. It is also a Site of Special Scientific Interest. Open from Easter to November, there is a Woodland Restaurant and Tearooms and a superb Gift Shop. Becky Falls will remain in your memory for ever.

Away to the south the great rocks known as BOWERMAN'S NOSE look like a petrified sentinel guarding the rugged hills, or a man with a sense of humour wearing a cardinal's hat playing God. Needless to say there is a legend about this strange, human looking column, which tells us how it came to be here. On this eastern part of the moor a tall, powerful giant of a man was known as Bowerman the Hunter. He loved the moors almost as much as he loved hunting. He kept a pack of large fierce hounds to aid this hobby. He was a jovial, kindly sort of man who was generous to the poor from his bag for the day and was liked almost by everyone who knew him, but there has to be an exception to the rule. In this case it was some of the many witches who held their meetings in hidden places on the moor and delighted in terrorising local people. Everyone was afraid of them except Bowerman. He was not even afraid of the Devil! He was their enemy and encouraged local people not to be afraid of the witches. In fact the witches were more than a little afraid of this big, strong man and his ferocious pack of hounds, themselves.

One day Bowerman and his dogs were chasing a hare which suddenly turned into a narrow valley with Bowerman in hot pursuit. It was in this valley that a coven of witches were holding their satanical Sabbath rites and they were not amused. Bowerman thought it funny and merely laughed at their weird rituals before he and his dogs continued their hunt. This was too much for the witches and they needed to seek revenge. One of the witches, Levara had the power to turn herself into a hare, and this she did.

Then she placed herself where Bowerman and his dogs would spot her, whilst the rest of the coven lay in ambush. Bowerman and his dogs had lost the original hare as they swept through the valley but now the dogs had picked up the scent of Levara who led them on a chase better than any Bowerman had ever experienced before. He was thrilled. It was not until he and his dogs were just about exhausted that Levara slowed down and allowed herself to be caught. At the same moment Bowerman found himself surrounded by a shrieking, howling mob of witches who combined their powers together to cast a spell which turned Bowerman and his hounds to stone.

The witches did not get away with it however. The people of Dartmoor were so angry, they forgot their fear and drove the witches out of Devon for ever. It is said that the witches knowing that they had upset so many people took to their broomsticks and allowed the wind to carry them across the Bristol Channel into Wales. Some say that is why many Welsh woman wear tall pointed witches hats!

There is another oddly named rock SPINSTER'S ROCK at SHILSTONE. It is the best known of the cromlechs or dolmens in Devon. Legend has it that three spinsters put it in place, but fact says it is the remains of a Neolithic tomb.

SPINSTERS ROCK

Whilst there are only two major roads which cross Dartmoor, the first from Plymouth to Moretonhampstead and the second from Tavistock to Ashburton, a number of ancient tracks and pathways exist as well as some more recent ones. This affords the visitor a wonderful opportunity for exploration. For those of us who are getting on a bit in years and find tough walks beyond our ability, the main roads provide many stopping places from which one can revel in the stunning views and venture for a stroll not too far away from one's vehicle. At least this gentle excercise allows one to inhale the wonderful, tangy air that always seems to me to be different from any other. In my younger days I walked THE ABBOTS WAY from CROSS FURZES near Buckfast Abbey to TAVISTOCK. Not an easy task because there is no definite route now and landmarks are few and far between. In medieval days the way would have been marked with granite crosses or humps of stones. Most of these have disappeared and if you want to follow this route you will need a map and a compass as well as a stout heart!

One of the best loved and most often told story of Dartmoor is about The Abbot's Way. The monks of both Buckfast and Tavistock Abbey were on good terms and frequently visited each other. This, as we know, was not an easy journey on foot. Between them lay bleak moorland, treacherous bogs, fast flowing streams and high tors which loomed above them. On the way the monks would stop sometimes at Plymstock Abbey, not so grand as the other two but nonetheless welcoming. Sadly Tavistock and Plymstock had a misunderstanding which developed into a totally un-Christian quarrel. Walter the Abbot of Tavistock decided it had to be resolved and he set out across the unwelcoming Abbot's Way to see what he could do. It was a case of while the cat's away the mice will play, although in this case it was four Tavistock monks, who seized the opportunity to make the most of their Abbot's absence. Whilst their fellow monks attended to the work of the Abbey, these four, rebelling against the austere life feasted and drank until they had exhausted every drop in the Abbot's wine cellar. Not satisfied they purchased more from Buckfastleigh to prolong their drinking spree. Luckily for them they were apprised that Walter, having patched up the quarrel with Plymstock had continued his journey to the Scilly Isles to inspect Abbey property there.

The drunken monks continued their orgy and one, Milbrosa, forgot himself so far as to steal the valuable silver communion vessels from the altar of the church and sell them to a band of passing gypsies. Once he sobered up he and his playfellows realised the enormity of what he had done. He implored his fellow monks to help him recover the stolen items. But what were they to do for money? Fortunately they knew a rich old Jew who owned a Blowing House - places where tin was smelted. Just as they arrived to see him, he was departing with a heavily laden pack horse. That the horse was laden with valuables they had no doubt, probably gold. They hid themselves away in a place where they knew the Jew would pass and as he did so they leapt out and overpowered him. Gold there was in plenty but not satisfied with this they committed the final sin by killing the old man and his trusty steed, and then threw them in a nearby bog so that no trace remained.

They thought they were safe from discovery, and having sought out the gypsies, and bought back the silver, they returned to the Abbey. Next morning they awoke to find the countryside covered in snow which made them feel even safer for it would conceal their inhuman act more thoroughly. Whilst they were having supper that evening a messenger arrived from the Abbot of Buckfast asking some of the monks to visit Buckfast because a miracle had happened and he and his Brothers wished to share it with them.

The journey was difficult, the messenger had set off ahead of them and by the time they had mounted their horses and ridden out, he was well ahead. They came up to him in the gathering gloom and stayed just behind him. The guide rode in silence. Suddenly a gap in the clouds let a piercing shaft of moonlight through, and the monks were terrified when they realised it was on the very spot where they had committed their heinous murder. Shaking in their saddles they gazed at each other and then at the guide who threw back his cowl. There was the old Jew, and as they watched, speechless and stunned, they saw the figure transformed into a spooky skeleton whose eyeless sockets bore into them. He stretched out his arm and with a bony finger, beckoned them to follow him. For a moment they hesitated but fear made them take the steps towards the outstretched arm straight into a deep bog. Within moments they and their horses had disappeared never to be seen again.

Abbot Walter had found out about their misdeeds but not the murder, and he was convinced they had been lost on the moor having missed the track. To prevent this happening again he ordered a number of granite crosses to be erected marking the path between the monasteries and at every one the monks were to stop and pray for the peace of the souls of the four missing monks.

When I am driving along the road from PLYMOUTH to TAVISTOCK I sometimes remind myself that this might well have been the route that Bronze Age men took. At the Plymouth end the route would have finished at a beach near Sutton Pool in the city. In fact all sorts of extraordinary thoughts go through my mind. Have you ever considered how difficult it must have been for mourners to take their loved ones on the last journey to church for burial? Imagine living in the depth of the moor and having to cart a coffin over the rough terrain for miles. No such a thing as an undertaker or a hearse. THE LICHWAY which runs from the eastern side of the moor to LYDFORD in the west was a famous track because much of Dartmoor lay within the Parish of Lydford and as such the only permitted burial place was Lydford church. It was rough and difficult to follow even on joyous occasions for weddings, baptisms and confirmations, so it must have been a journey of misery for those already grief-stricken.

Lydford

CHAPTER ONE - DARTMOOR NATIONAL PARK

So many stories are applicable to Dartmoor and whilst I am writing about LYDFORD, it is a good moment to tell you about the place. Firstly LYDFORD GORGE is an unsurpassed beauty spot, now in the care of the National Trust. Water pours off the moor onto its boulders with a ferocity that would overshadow a witches cauldron. It was home once to a band of villainous red-bearded robbers with the unlikely name of Gubbins, led by Roger Rowle, the self-styled Robin Hood of the West, whose story Kingsley told in 'Westward Ho'. They brought misery to the village and trepidation to travellers. Good does come out of evil however. Debauchery, intemperance and inter-breeding brought their reign of terror to an end; they disappeared. Today you can stand on the little footbridge looking 300ft down the gorge and see nothing but nature at its most beautiful and mysterious.

Alfred the Great had a hand in the founding of Lydford. It was one of his four moorland burghs and was sited on a hill overlooking the river Lyd. Less than a mile downstream it was possible to ford the river - and so the name Lydford. The Danes burnt it down in AD997, probably because of the mint which was operating and producing coins known as Lydford Pennies, some of which are still in existence and can be seen in the 16th century CASTLE INN, a favourite haunt of mine.

The inn is one of those snug, country pubs that welcomes you instantly. You can stay in one of its well-appointed rooms, some of which look over Dartmoor and the others over the garden. Downstairs the bars are warm and attractive and in one, The Foresters, meals are served amidst low lamp-lit beams, a vast collection of old plates, and a great Norman fireplace ablaze with logs in winter. If you enquire you will discover that the stones of the fireplace are Norman but it was not built in this time. The stones were nicked from the castle! It is in this bar that you can see some Lydford Pennies. Bar meals are served at lunchtime as well as in the evenings. Every night the a la carte restaurant is open for business and has a wide menu which majors on local produce. It is as well to book a table.

I always expect the inn to be haunted but as far as I know there has never been a sighting. However when you consider the appalling things that happened in the castle it is surprising that no spirit took refuge in the bar. All that remains of the castle now is the keep, but for a long time it was used as a prison for Stannary Law offenders. These tinners had the so-called privilege of being tried by their fellow tradesmen under the unique Lydford Law dispensed in the courts which were in being long after it was no longer necessary to take bodies to Lydford for burial. Quite horrendous was the manner in which the law was administered. More often than not the offender was hung, drawn and quartered in the morning and the trial held in the afternoon. What if the offender was innocent? You can sense the evil surrounding the remains of the castle even today. You will never see a bird; they have an inborn alarm system that steers them away from evil.

The church is older than the castle, and stems from the 7th century but it is mainly 15th century. Inside it safeguards the old village stocks and has the most wonderful bench ends to be found anywhere, some 69 in all. Carved with every conceivable flower, bird, fish and animal, they are a joy. There is even one presented to the church by King Edward VIII which has a figure of Edward the Confessor holding a model of Westminster Abbey. The fine oak screen, with a fan-vaulted canopy, is in memory of Daniel Radford, who restored the church and made the gorge accessible.

If you wander round the churchyard you will spot some very ancient headstones and on one just outside the main door of the church, a fascinating epitaph to George Routleigh, watchmaker:

'He had the art of disposing of his time so well that
his hours glided away in one continual round of pleasure
and delight till an unlucky minute put a period to his existence.'

Having once more wandered off my plotted path for this chapter I am going to return to the question of burials but first I must tell you the story of a strange Dartmoor custom which existed up to the mid-19th century. On Dartmoor if a house could be built, with a roof in place, between sunrise and sunset, then the house and all the land around it became the builder's. The only such cottage I know that still exists is Jolly Lane Cot at HUCCABY near Hexworthy.

Tom and Sally Satterly chose Midsummer's Day to set about their task and by sunset they had succeeded. This meant that they were free from bonded employment. In her later years Sally used to be seen sitting in her front doorway talking to passersby and frequently singing old folk songs. She knew so many that Sabine Baring Gould who wrote 'Onward Christian Soldiers' and of whom I will write more presently, made a special trip to visit her and write down the songs for posterity.

On Sally's death the male mourners carried her coffin across the tors to WIDECOMBE for burial and rested their burden en route on the last remaining coffin stone on the moor. So it was not only along the Lichway that these tortuous and unhappy journeys were carried out.

There is a Dartmoor legend which I am told can be attributed to Sally Satterly although there is no written evidence that it is about her. I like to think it so because it fits in with the pattern of her life. Anyway, folk will tell you that when she sat in her pretty garden she attracted many children and she also became friendly with the animals and birds that wandered and flew in. In the winter she always made sure that there was food and water put out for them. In the spring and summer her garden was ablaze with flowers and one night she awoke from sleep quite sure that she could hear music outside. When she looked out of her window she was astounded to see her lawn full of dancing pixies. Even more amazing was the sight of her tulips swaying in time with the music. When she looked more closely she saw that the cup of each tulip cradled a tiny, sleeping pixie baby. From that time onwards Sally always paid especial attention to the tulips and wove many a story for the children when they came to call.

Also at Hexworthy in the quiet of the Swincombe valley is WYDEMEET FARMHOUSE, a beautiful and secluded granite house built early this century. It is in Dartmoor's solitude that so many secrets are hidden and that is why a super couple, Jan and Kevin Chamberlain, run MOUNTAIN STREAM ACTIVITIES from Wydemeet.

If you enjoy the challenge and excitement of outdoor pursuits as well as loving the ruggedness of the moors, you will not find a better holiday than the one on offer here. Amongst the many choices are climbing and abseiling for which the Tors, rivers and seacliffs of the area provide a wide variety of climbs suitable for the novice or the experienced. Safety is obviously vitally important and all the specialist equipment is maintained to a very high standard. Everyone must wear a protective helmet and will always be secured by a safety rope. Kevin also ensures that there is an appropriate pupil/instructor ratio.

You must be sure to bring a windproof jacket if you want to go canoeing, which is very exciting. You are taken out either, on the river, down to the coast or to a local reservoir. You need not worry if you are totally inexperienced; the instructors have infinite patience.

One of the best attributes of this splendid holiday is being taught the correct way to navigate across the wild moorland, learning about all the correct equipment to carry, and the techniques involved in route planning and orienteering. You can go on an expedition that will last up to a week and include camping.

Orienteering, for those who wish to become extremely proficient and enjoy a challenge, is another planned activity. These courses are of varying difficulty and great fun. It is one good way of trying to seek out some of the famous Dartmoor 'Letter-boxes'.

These are just a few of the activities that Mountain Stream offers. Staying at Wydemeet completes the picture. Do not expect luxurious accommodation because what is on offer is a sturdy bunk bed in a large bedroom which you may share with anything from four to eight people. Adjoining the bedrooms there are separate shower, washing and toilet facilities. Downstairs there is a large, comfortable dining room and lounge which have roaring log fires and spectacular views of the moors.

It is just as well that there is so much physical activity because Jan Chamberlain's food is wholesome and filling. You will never leave the table hungry.

A recent addition has been a centrally-heated chalet which adjoins the farmhouse and is available as a self-catering unit for up to 16 people. This has been designed with easy access in mind for disabled people who are made very welcome. To get further details on this excellent venture you will find information in the back of this book.

My mention of Sabine Baring Gould allows me to tell you about his home at LEWTRENCHARD just a mile or so from Lydford. It is a quiet and lovely place tucked in the valley of the River Lew. Hidden in the woods is the 15th-century church so tiny that it seems to be full of benches and a fine old screen. Sabine Baring Gould was rector here for 43 years and he was in his ninetieth year when he was laid to rest in the churchyard in 1924. This compassionate, well travelled man gave so much to the world apart from the restoration of this lovely church and his never to be forgotten stirring hymns. There is one story told about him which I feel is a little sad but it illustrates the lifestyle of the man who was so often away from home. A little girl stood in the door of the church and smiled up at him. He looked benevolently down on her and said 'Who are you'? 'I am your daughter, Papa' came the answer. He was a bit like Mother Hubbard; he had so many children he didn't know who was who! His home was LEWTRENCHARD MANOR now a superb country house hotel, small enough with its eight beautifully appointed bedrooms, to give one the sense of being part of a house party. It is the home of James and Sue Murray who are the sort of people who would make anyone feel at ease and at home whevererver they resided, and this talent they brought to Lewtrenchard some seven years ago. These years have been to put to good use in slowly, lovingly and painstakingly bringing the house back to its original glory.

It is a house that I find entrancing especially the long gallery which runs the length of the central part of the house. There are sofas everywhere, more panelling and yet another wonderful ceiling. It is here at Christmas that the carol singers come to sing round the piano and afterwards tuck

LEWTRENCHARD MANOR

into the punch and hot home-made mincepies. The enchanting ballroom is full of collectors items brought back by Sabine Baring Gould from his travels. He was an impulsive collector and what intriques me more than anything else is the difficulties he must have encountered bringing all his finds back to Lewtrenchard. The ornate wood carving from Bavaria for example, which is installed in the ballroom. You may think it slightly over the top with its wealth of floral carving that trails from the floor to the ceiling, alongside and over the fireplace, until it joins the equally decorative plaster figures above one's head. It reminded me of an Austrian concert hall.

In the Hall which is vast and has a welcoming, open fireplace, the mantelpiece is a fine, probably medieval, carved panel, held up by two beautifully carved Victorian pieces of mahogany. It does not offend in the least; Sabine, even if he did forget his children, had a genius for putting the right things together.

The house was built about 1620 on the site of an earlier dwelling recorded in the Domesday book. It has a strange history but you can feel the mantle of love enveloping it. It was the childhood home of General George Monk, first Duke of Albemarle, who, himself, had some tough times before he found fame and fortune, much like the house which for years in this century lay empty before it was let to tenants and during World War 11 to billet Army Officers. Several people had a shot at turning it into an hotel but they were unsuccessful, mainly because they had neither a love for the house nor an understanding of the business. It was good fortune for all those who discover Lewtrenchard Manor either to stay in or to enjoy a super meal, that James and Sue Murray decided to leave South Africa where they were farmers, and acquire the Manor for the sole purpose of turning it into the first class home and establishment it is today.

To continue the story of General George Monk, In 1626 his father was forced to sell the Manor to a relative, Henry Gould, in order to raise money to get his son out of prison, to which he had been condemned by Cromwell. The most famous member of the family was Sabine Baring Gould.

Lewtrenchard Manor would make an excellent base, not at the cheap end of the market, for those who would like to explore Dartmoor and return at night to this fabulous house and a superb dinner before retiring to sleep in the greatest comfort, in a room named after one of Sabine's hymns. 'Now the Day is Over' perhaps?

Everywhere on the moor there are tracks, some going nowhere apparently and some of comparatively modern construction. Many of thes tracks have been formed over centuries and the deepest and most worn are probably where men continuously walked when they went out to cut peat or to take cattle to good grazing land. Peat was virtually the only fuel of moorland farmers and once the peat was cut it was taken back to the farms, stacked and dried ready for use in the cold winter. You will find some of the more recent ones marked at each end by granite posts, some of which are dedicated to individuals.

Peat not only provides fuel, it is capable of holding vast quantities of water and in so doing prevents flooding. Towns and villages were supplied from Dartmoor water sources since the 16th century. PLYMOUTH was the first and it was Sir Francis Drake who constructed a leat from Dartmoor to the town. This was completed in 1591. DEVONPORT, now part of Plymouth, was the next, some two hundred years later. There is still evidence of these leats in Plymouth today. Dartmoor via its damns, pipes and reservoirs now supplies most of the surrounding area with water.

BURRATOR was the first dam to be built on High Dartmoor and the ensuing reservoir not only serves a utilitarian purpose but has provided visitors and local people with a superb place to visit. You can walk all the way round it enjoying magical views, sometimes high and sometimes low. The colouring changes with every season but it will never fail to give you great pleasure. There are a number of places to park around the reservoir but toilets are located near the dam. If you feel in need of refreshment during your walk you will find friendly refreshment vans parked at the Dam and at Norsworthy Bridge. FERNWORTHY is another reservoir, near Chagford which I mention in the chapter on Chagford. The MELDON reservoir is near Okehampton. From the dam there are good views south to the high moor and northwards down the West

Okement Valley. Not the place to be in winter; it is very exposed. Then there are the smaller VENFORD and AVON DAM Reservoirs near Holne. All meeting the insatiable water demands of the growing populace. One of my favourite walks is at the Avon Dam. From the car park at Shipley Bridge there is not a bad road which takes you to its foot. The walk is about two and a half miles along a route which rises gently but is delightful and if you feel a bit puffed there are plenty of places along the river bank where you can rest.

BURRATOR

Letter-boxing is a pastime that has become increasingly popular and gives many people hours of pleasure searching for them. I understand that today there are some 3,000 of them. Many Conservationists will say 3,000 too many. Dartmoor Letter-boxes are fairly recent and came about when a Dartmoor guide named James Perrot left a box at CRANMERE POOL for the purpose of visitors leaving visiting cards and signing a visitors book. Many more 'drops' have copied the idea although some of them are very isolated and hard to find including what is said to be the 'Mecca' of Dartmoor Post Boxes at FUR TOR. The object today is to use the letter-boxes for postcards which having been addressed and stamped with the official stamp you leave behind for the next visitor. You take away with you whatever mail you find on your arrival. Just to keep you on your toes it is quite likely that you will find a clue which will lead you to the next letter-box. Half the fun is seeing how long it takes to receive mail this way! It is almost like a never ending treasure hunt. A word of warning, the old idea of letter boxing was fine but today people seem to create new boxes, not caring how much damage they might do to the environment.

Some of the so-called letterboxes are super market shopping bags! Perhaps, if you truly love the moor you should take note of the great country writer Richard Jefferies who said, 'Where man goes, nature ends'. If you would like more information on letter-boxing there are booklets to be had at the information centres which will reveal all, and the code of conduct for users.

To those of us who live within the confines of the city, the world of the farmer on Dartmoor seems to be romantic but in reality it is a harsh life. Sheep graze peacefully across the moor but they all have to be brought in to be dipped against scab. On a fine day it is magical to watch the sheepdogs at work aided by a few people on horseback whose task is to steer the animals into pens. It all seems so simple but it still has to be done when the weather is at its worst! Animals have to be fed no matter what the wind or rain may do. Most farms do not have grid fed electricity and are dependent on their own generators. The farmers wife cannot hop along to the super-market for something she has forgotten or run out of. It is a world of its own, beloved by those whose lifestyle it is but no one will say it is easy.

That bone of contention, Fox hunting, raises its head on Dartmoor where four packs hunt and there are a lot of foxes. I have no strong opinion either way. I enjoy the spectacle of the hunt, the colour and the cheerful banter over the stirrup cups at a meet. I dislike any form of cruelty but I do know what an opportunist the fox is. Some kill lambs, most do damage of some kind and it is understandable that the farming community demands that they are kept down. What we do not hear about so much is the shooting and trapping of the foxes. Is that a better death than a kill by a hound whose weight will be considerably heavier than its quarry? The hound will go for the neck and kill almost immediately. Something to think about. Most hunting folk are there for the thrill of the gallop across wide open spaces and certainly have a love of animals.

Compared to the fox I think it is the badger who has been subjected to unbelievable cruelty for centuries. This is a cause dear to the heart of Ruth Murray whose Badger Sanctuary at Laughter Hole, Postbridge is a haven for these poor creatures. Ruth's knowledge of badgers is vast and recognised world wide. Never one to mince her words, she has strong views on protection. Her sanctuary started when she became sickened by the evil baiting gangs who seemed to be in league with the Ministry of Agriculture's wholesale slaughter policy. Laughter Hole is not open to the public but that does not stop people visiting from all over the world. The law at the moment does not permit the return of badgers to the outside world, and so many of these beautiful animals have come to know Laughter Hole as their permanent home. I have no doubt there would be some idiots who would shout loudly that keeping animals penned is wrong but surely this is preferable to leaving the poor things to badger baiting. Ruth Murray is not the only one on the moor caring for badgers. There is a very active Dartmoor Badgers' Protection League who set out in all weathers to confront those who would destroy setts or trap the animals.

At the back of this book you will find a list of publications which will aid those of you who wish to dig more deeply into specialist subjects. I have to keep a firm rein on myself to prevent dipping into these books and getting so fascinated that I lose track of the purpose of this out-pouring of words!

The only way to help you discover and delight in all that there is to see and do within the 365 square miles of Dartmoor is to take you on a roundabout tour which, because I live in Plymouth, starts on the edge of the moor at CLEARBROOK, a small hamlet, about halfway between Yelverton and Meavy. It takes its name from the sparkling clear brook which runs the whole way through the bottom of the long gardens at the back of the row of cottages. Its accumulation of water comes from the moor and from a myriad of springs. I wondered why a hamlet sprang up in what appears to be the middle of nowhere. A little digging, and I discovered that the cottages were built in 1880 by tin miners who were employed at the Yeoland Console Mine which had been in operation since the middle of the 18th century. It was reputedly one of the most productive mines in the area. It certainly was the first to úse a water turbine, the water coming from Drake's leat which as I had discovered before, was built by Sir Francis Drake in 1591 to take water from Burrator to Plymouth.

The River Meavy runs through the hamlet and divides the two parishes of Meavy and Yelverton. On the Meavy side there are two miner's cottages, built in the 16th century which are under a preservation order. The focal point of this small hamlet is a lively hostelry, THE SKYLARK, popular both locally and with the many people who stream out from Plymouth onto the moor at the weekends especially. Here you will find good company, good ale and good, reasonably priced pub fare.

Like so many small places Clearbrook has no shop and no church but today the miners cottages and what are known as a block of 'town houses' built in 1890, are inhabited largely by people who travel the 20 minutes into Plymouth to their work.

MEAVY is far more of a village, complete with a village green, and THE ROYAL OAK INN, whose landlords are none other than the parish. It is a pub of character which was originally built in the 12th century as a church house, and then was rebuilt in the 18th century. In spite of this it is still a welcoming country pub as good in winter as it is in summer. Although I have to confess I enjoy most a drink in summer sitting outside on the green, close to the ancient Meavy Oak which is probably about 500 years old and has, like so many oldies, the need for iron beam supports. When it does finally go, as it must, there is a sturdy young oak already growing to continue the tradition. St Peter's church beside the green is said to have been given to the villagers by Cnut the Dane, or at least permission to build a church, but the present church dates from Norman times with much rebuilding in the 13th and 15th centuries. The Drake door in the south wall which was added in 1705, allowed the Lady Chapel to be used as a family pew. It is a church that is redolent of faith and the loving care given to it by its parishioners. In June the annual Meavy Oak Fair is held, a happy occasion, when there is fun for everyone but be prepared to find a parking place for your car quite a long way off.

Between Meavy and BICKLEIGH, with its old bridge over the Plym, a village green, and a fine pinnacled and much loved church, well over 500 years old, is SHAUGH PRIOR, standing above its bridge which is a popular beauty spot owned by the National Trust. It has sheer rocks and the much climbed DEWERSTONE closeby and has been used many times by film makers.

The main road from Plymouth to Yelverton has many diversionary side roads, excellent for walkers and cyclists. To the left is the winding road that leads down to the beautiful LOPWELL DAM, a favourite with everyone. A little further on is the turning for BERE ALSTON and BERE FERRERS which I will tell you about in a minute but first of all let me introduce you to one of my favourite hotels in Devon, THE MOORLAND LINKS, clearly signposted from the main road. This was the haunt of my youth, and where during the war every Saturday night we danced the night away to the music of Frankie Fuge and his band - a name that will conjure up memories for many. One must remember that Plymouth was a Garrison city as well as a Naval port with the result that every arm of the services would be represented. The men resplendent in uniform, the girls frequently in long dresses which had been made from old curtain material discovered in attics! It was wonderful then, and I have loved it ever since although one can hardly compare the standard of the food! Today it has been superbly refurbished, new bedrooms added; the Gunroom Bar is a friendly meeting place. The restaurant looks out over the pretty gardens and beyond is the ballroom still much in demand, and used for all sorts of functions. It is a hotel equipped to look after the individuals who come to stay perhaps for a weekend break, or for a wedding reception, product launch or conference. Run by one of the best hoteliers in the country, Graham Jenkins, and supported by an able staff, I wholeheartedly recommend it.

MOORLAND LINKS HOTEL

Just before you come to Yelverton there is a turn to the left which will bring you to THE HARROWBEER COUNTRY HOUSE HOTEL, the ideal spot for someone in the area on business to unwind at night or for families to stay, enjoy the magic of Dartmoor, and the wonder of the South Devon coastline. It is owned by a delightful couple, Ron and Patsy Back whose aim is to ensure your well being. You will find it both comfortable, relaxing and not wildly expensive.

Your pets will be very welcome and free of charge. All that is asked of you is to leave a donation for the local animal rescue. Delicious home-cooked meals are always available for residents, and by prior arrangement for non-residents. There is a comfortable lounge but it does sometimes get neglected because everyone tends to congregate in the bar area which has an enormous log fire apart from some excellent whisky!

Harrowbeer House was an R.A.F. Officers' Mess during the war when Harrabeer was an airfield housing fighter squadrons. I was engaged to one of the pilots and so I knew it well. You may be amazed when I tell you that 193 Squadron who flew Typhoons from here, had a duck as their mascot. Every night it accompanied its masters to the pub, usually The Royal Oak at Meavy. Here the duck would get its beak into any beer mug and frequently ended up absolutely pixilated. I was led to understand that it never suffered a hangover!

From here YELVERTON is just a stone's throw away A village which is split by a main road but nonetheless has much to offer. A parade of shops offering everything from a supermarket to a butcher and chemist, plus a bank or two, runs alongside a good pub, THE ROCK INN. This is an interesting pub which was originally a farmhouse and later a coaching house. The building has been owned by the same family since 1894. The inn became a link via horse drawn railway, between Yelverton and Princetown, when Dartmoor prison was built. At one time The Rock was an hotel but today a complex has been built up around the inn consisting of a dentist, accountant, solicitor, hairdresser, clothes shop and a taxi company. Every taste is catered for in the pub. Good wholesome, Daily Specials, grace the menu and whether you are a good trencherman, a child or a Vegetarian, the food will please.

The second part of Yelverton is known as LEG O'MUTTON CORNER. It is a little world of its own separated from the main body of the village by the main Tavistock Road. It is complete with a pub, a newsagent which sells almost anything, the excellent JASMINE CHINESE RESTAURANT, which also has a Take-Away service, a tearoom and my favourite place THE YELVERTON PAPERWEIGHT CENTRE.

My first visit some years back opened my eyes to the beauty and magic of paperweights. It was the radiance of the colours that first struck me. Everywhere there were well-lit cabinets and showcases, housing these superb objects. Once I had taken in the overall spectacle I wanted to know more about the individual pieces and who better to tell me than the owner Kay Bolster.

Hers is an interesting story. Originally she worked with her present right-hand woman, Susan Portchmouth, for Bernard Broughton, whose collection forms the base of the centre. He was an incredible man who first started showing his collection in St Tudy, a small Cornish village, in 1968, and later moved to Yelverton. His love for these beautiful objects and for the history of paperweights rubbed off onto Kay, who had little knowledge at all when she started working for him. It was her instinctive love of beautiful things which had surrounded her in her formative years, that developed in the years they worked together. When he died, Kay bought this unique business, and with the invaluable help of Susan, she has built a tremendous following all over the world. These two charming and knowledgeable ladies will talk to anyone and make a point of doing so, showing the uninitiated like myself some of the facets of the world of paperweights.

The Yelverton Paperweight Centre celebrated its Silver Jubilee last year. The collection has grown considerably since it started, and now has some 800 paperweights on permanent exhibition, reputed to be the largest private collection in Europe. Among them are many from the factories of Baccarat and St Louis who make the finest French paperweights. Both the casual visitor and serious collector are fascinated by the beautifully handcrafted Millefiori and abstract designs.

I fell in love with the Millefiori weights, which consist of a great variety of ends of fancy canes cut sectionally, at right angles with the filigree cane to form small lozenges or tablets. These, when placed side by side, and massed by transparent glass, have the appearance of a series of flowers or rosettes. If you think I have suddenly become an expert on paperweights, I have to confess I am cheating! When I left the Paperweight Centre, I was so enthralled by what I had seen that I read avidly about this unique art form.

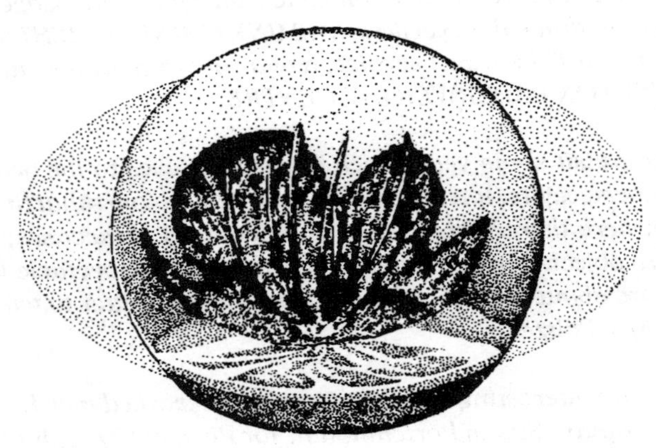

PAPERWEIGHT CENTRE

Collecting paperweights need not be a costly business, although the most expensive one in the world was sold for £99,000 in 1990. Here one can start from the modest price of a fiver rising to somewhere over £1600.

As far as I can discover there is not another Paperweight Centre to rival this one in the whole of the country. It attracts collectors from all over the world. Admission is completely free and so is parking.

If your tastes are for equestrian sport then I readily commend CROSSWAYS RIDING SCHOOL in Axtown Lane, Yelverton. This well established business was once a racing yard. Alex Howard and her husband, Bob, bought it in 1984 and have steadily developed it into the well thought of school it is today. The Howards both have a love of horses and people, although I am not sure that the horses do not take precedence! They have twenty five horses, with school horses and liveries.

Dartmoor gives a lot of option to the rider, depending on the weather, the time of the year and the level of skill the pupil has. Alex likes to think that Crossways is a riding school with old fashioned values, not a trekking centre as so many stables are. Crossways gives instruction to BHSS exam level and has working pupils training for their certificates.

As well as themselves, the Howards have two qualified instructors in their staff of six. It is very much a team, all working together for the good of the horses and the stable. People are made very welcome and not in the least cliquey as so often happens in the horsey world. They are particularly good with new and nervous people as well as small children.

I was interested to find that Crossways has 'Stable Days' in which people are introduced to the art and skill of stable management rather than riding. It is very popular and quite rightly so with such professional people running it. The art of riding side-saddle has come into its own again and here you can get instruction in this elegant style. Several of the Crossway horses can carry side-saddles, and a visiting instructor is available. If you are worried about making a fool of yourself if you have never ridden before, you truly do not have to worry here. They are practical, sympathetic and will laugh with you rather than at you.

One important role Crossways plays is through the South Dartmoor group of Riding for the Disabled Association. The stable offers both riding and driving instruction. We are talking about traps, not cars, incidentally. One trap is specially adapted to take a wheelchair. Lessons for the able-bodied who want to drive a trap, are also available. I learnt that before a pony can qualify for use by the disabled he has to be put through a two hour test.

You will find a good many riding schools and stables on Dartmoor and for reference purposes you will find a list at the back of this book. I obviously cannot write about them all at length.

A little further on from Yelverton is the charming village of BUCKLAND MONACHORUM with a super pub, THE DRAKE MANOR INN, standing adjacent to a picturesque 15th century church with superbly carved choir stalls bursting with angels and acorns and berries. Of great interest is a bench-end in the Drake Chapel, built by Sir Francis but rebuilt in the next generation. It has a shield with a ship on the top of a globe, the Golden Hind, in which Drake sailed round the world.

THE DRAKE MANOR INN

The pub is beloved by local people and visitors who have discovered it over the years. A babbling brook flows gently by the beer garden; idyllic for drinks on a summer day. Part of this ancient building may date back to the 12th century, when it is believed to have been a monks hostelry. The local story is that it was first built to house the masons and workmen who erected the church, and thereafter, became a Pilgrims' inn. Bar snacks and full meals are available daily. The emphasis is on good, wholesome home-cooking. Are you a lover of malt whiskies? There are over thirty in stock!

Run by The Fortescue Garden Trust, THE GARDEN HOUSE is a delight. The walled garden has been described as 'the most beautiful one and a half acres in England.' It is no exaggeration. From March to October the colour is brilliant, with an enormous range of plants on view. Teas and lunches are served in the main rooms of the elegant house. There is a well stocked plant centre, which has an enviable reputation as a source of well-grown unusual plants. You will find it open every day from March to October between 10.30am and 5pm.

Buckland Monachorum has in its keeping one of Devon's treasures, BUCKLAND ABBEY the beloved home of Sir Francis Drake. On the floor are still the tiles that Drake and Grenville walked on, for Buckland Abbey was the home of both. Drake has always been one of my heroes and so I commend this 13th century Cistercian monastery to everyone. There was a time when it looked as though it might have been a gem lost to us forever for just before World War 11, fire broke out in one of its wings and ruined it from floor to roof. However all is now well and you may delight in the beauty of this exquisite place and its grounds.

Drake lived here for the last fifteen years of his life and you can see many relics of this greatest of all seamen. In a case in the Great Hall stands Drake's Drum which was with him when he died at sea in 1596. It was the beating of this drum that called sailors to battle. I can almost hear the sound of the steady, insistent beat as sailors tumbled on to the deck of the Revenge ready to take on the Spanish Armada. Documents concerning the Armada are to be seen as well as Drake's will written in a shaky, almost illegible hand the night before he died. There too is the silver-cased compass inscribed with precise points on the Spanish Main and the ports of Europe. I wonder how often Drake took this little treasure from his pocket to stir his memory of some great day in his life. Even in dark days the little line on the silver map must have given him courage.

BUCKLAND ABBEY

Drake was acutely aware of the power that wealth brought, as indeed were most of the buccaneering Elizabethans. He acquired vast estates. Elizabeth I gave him the manor of Sherford, between Plympton and Elburton, now part of Plymouth and in the same year, 1582, he purchased part of the manor at Yarcombe from the Drakes of Ash.

By the time of his second marriage, he had added the manor of Sampford Spiney to the rest of his property. This lovely old manor house is now in the hands of one of Drake's descendants, Andrew Spedding and his wife Ros, good friends of mine. 'Spud' Spedding is well known to the sailing fraternity throughout the world, and I detect in him something of the spirit of Drake. His adventures would make a book in themselves as I am sure his friends would agree. He is the sort of man who knows people all over the world, in every walk of life and if ever you need something, he might not personally have the answer but he will certainly know a man who does!

These properties stayed within the Drake Abbey estate until the first break up of the West Devon part in 1942. Fortunately in 1946, when Buckland Abbey came on the market, Plymouth found a benefactor in Captain Arthur Rudd, a Yelverton landowner who came forward to buy the Abbey and then gave it to the National Trust. The gift was conditional. The Abbey had to be restored and, on completion, the City of Plymouth should take over responsibility of opening the Abbey to the public as a Drake Naval and West Country Folk Museum. It is much in use today for far more than visitors wandering round. Delightful concerts are held here as well as many other functions.

There are several villages within easy reach of Yelverton. The little, close knit community at MILTON COMBE where the village pub, THE WHO'D HAVE THOUGHT IT INN is a favourite hostelry for people from many miles around. It is the friendliest of places, full of old world charm. You will find the food is good pub fare of a very high standard but at the same time sensibly priced. In the summer one has the added bonus of being able to sit outside on the terrace in totál peace which is only disturbed by the gurgling of the stream that runs alongside. I have always found it to be a great place to seek refreshment after a visit to closeby, Buckland Abbey. There is something about historical places that engender a thirst! Lopwell Dam is another beauty spot just down the road.

The criteria that I always apply to inns, is the number of local people and others who use it regularly. If they do you can be sure it will be worth visiting. Here, at the Who'd Have Thought It, you will always find them gathered round the bar, enjoying the well-kept ale and the cheerful banter that goes with familiarity. Certainly an establishment to put on your visiting list. If you wonder how it acquired its name, there are several stories but the most likely seems to be one that appeared in the Western Evening Herald. This states that the lexicographer, Samuel Johnson was walking on the moor one day when he stopped for a breather at a bridge which overlooked Milton Combe. A local yokel was standing there too and having passed the time of the day with him, Johnson asked if there was an inn nearby where he could get some refreshment. The yokel replied ' There's one just below you. If you look over the bridge you can look down the chimney.' To which Dr Johnson answered, 'Well, who'd have thought it.'

Country Premises

WALKHAMPTON for example has its pub, THE WALKHAMPTON INN. Not much in the village to attract the visitor, but the pub is comfortable and friendly and has a garden that is a sun trap in summer. On the main road just by the turning to Walkhampton, is THE BURRATOR INN at Dousland. I have never felt it to be a very welcoming place from outside but walk through the doors and you are within the portals of a happy, lively establishment which seems to be busy every day of the week and does just about everything. From Monday to Saturday inclusive it is open from 11am-11pm during which time you can sample everything from morning coffee, a good bar snack - they make a particularly good Seafood Chowder - to afternoon cream teas with freshly baked scones and real Devonshire Clotted Cream and home-made jams, as well as strawberries and cream in season. The restaurant has a goodly selection of dishes, and every Thursday night there is Country and Western Music. Every weekend there seems to be some kind of live entertainment. Comfortable en-suite accommodation is also available. Families are especially welcome and there is a large car park.

SHEEPSTOR close to Burrator is merely a collection of houses in a wonderful, moorland setting. Please do drive carefully; the road is very narrow. One of these once belonged to the white Rajah of Sarawak and has an entrancing water garden. The romantic story of the two men of the Brooke family who became rulers of Sarawak always appeals to me. They both lie buried in the 15th century churchyard at Sheepstor, a constant reminder of two men who devoted their lives to the people of Sarawak to whom they brought peace and prosperity.

James Brooke was born in India in 1804 whilst his father was serving there. He was sent back to England to be educated but returned to India at the age of 16 as a cadet in the infantry. After one battle he was left for dead but saved by a friend. It took him so long to recover that the Army had no further use for him. After his father died he inherited £30,000, a fortune in those days. Uncertain of what he wanted to do, he bought a yacht and set sail for nowhere in particular. In 1839 he reached Sarawak to find a civil war in progress. His help was readily given to repel the revolt and in gratitude he was asked to remain and become the ruler of the province. The mixed bag of races did not make this an easy task. He had to contend with Christians, Chinese, Malays, Moslems, and worst of all, head hunters.

He struggled for years against piracy and head hunting, spending his own fortune to establish a land which was peaceful and prosperous. The British Government did not want to know but he did find one ally in Baroness Burdett-Coutts, a member of the banking family. She was in love with him and is believed to have proposed marriage, which he rejected but he did not reject the money she loaned him when he was penniless. He always repaid his debts. By 1852 he had just about achieved his goal when his nephew Charles, who was ex-Royal Navy, came out to join him. Charles was persuaded to change his surname of Johnson to Brooke and carried on the name and the work.

Sarawak was still a volatile place and in 1857 the Chinese sacked the capital, Kuching. It caught Sir James unawares and he escaped by plunging into the river and swimming away in the dark. To the rescue came Charles and with a force of Malays and Dyaks beat off the Chinese.

Sir James died at Sheepstor in 1868 and Charles took over in Sarawak. There can have been no stranger or more prosperous community anywhere in the world. He managed to educate his unruly pirates and headhunters, provide schools, roads, a railway, waterworks, telegraph, telephone and radio. By now the British Government was only too ready to acquire Sarawak as a Protectorate.

Charles came back to Sheepstor for a holiday in 1917 and it was here he died and lies at rest not far from his uncle, under a rough moorland stone.

BERE ALSTON and BERE FERRERS are two villages between Yelverton and Tavistock. Bere Alston is the more commercial of the two and is a busy place with a populace that either works locally, in Tavistock, or commutes to Plymouth. One man who has his flourishing business at 17 Chapel Street is Glyn Berrington. THE BERRINGTON DRAUGHTING AND TECHNICAL SERVICES offer a wide range of facilities to anyone wanting small or large projects undertaken. The company will cope with anything from factory extensions to Atrium roofs, fire escapes to portal frame buildings. In fact whatever your drawing requirements are, Glyn will do his best to satisfy your needs. This is a man with many hidden talents not the least of them his vast knowledge of bee keeping. He is the Chairman of the Tavistock Bee Keepers Association and it is his enthusiasm for the science that is instrumental in the increasing number of people who are taking part in this skilled and fascinating hobby.

I have always found Bere Alston friendly but a slightly grey place and preferred the delightful Bere Ferrers which is designated an area of outstanding natural beauty and lies on a peninsula bordered by the rivers Tavy and Tamar, 15 miles from Plymouth. The name 'bere' is Celtic and means narrow strip of land. So Bere followed by Ferrers indicates the name of the lords of the manor whose demesne it was. For 200 years it was the most highly specialised mining community in Southern England. Bere silver had its own stamp and in the 14th century mines were reserved for the King's exclusive use. The rivers played their part in the prosperity of Bere Ferrers; they were the main link for the import of timber,lime and coal and for the export of minerals, fruit and flowers. Apart from mining the people of the Tamar valley have always been engaged in horticulture. The mild climate and south facing slopes are ideal for the early production of fruit and flowers. Today there are less farms but a vineyard - Birlanda -flourishes, concentrating on the white wines Schonburger and Riesling.

The charming village cottages of white-washed stone and cob are to be found in Silver Street which once was known as Duck Alley. The small and busy main street boasts a post office and an inn. Much has clearly been renovated and designed but none of the attractiveness has disappeared, and several of the properties can be dated back to the 16th or early 17th century.

The pride of the village is St Andrew's church sitting on the bank of the river Tavy. It was built by Sir William de Ferrers about 1258 and rebuilt less than a hundred years later by his grandson William, who established a collegiate church with five priests. They were to pray for William and his wife Matilda in perpetuity. He installed rare stained glass from France in the east window, showing himself and his wife offering the church to the Lord. This you can still see today and further afield in Exeter Cathedral there are some examples of this, the oldest glass in Devon. Other notable features of the interior include a late Norman girdle-tub font, the base of a late medieval panelled rood screen, a late 15th century wooden ceiling with fine carved bosses in the porch, and some Elizabethan carved bench ends.

It was community spirit that saved this beautiful church from ruin. In 1979 St Andrew's was said to be beyond repair and the Church Commissioners wanted to declare it redundant. The 250 or so villagers rebelled against this idea and decided to restore their church. It took them nine years to raise the money by every conceivable fund raising exercise which together with help from English Heritage gave them eighty thousand pounds; enough for the restoration. It is a tribute to Bere Ferrers and a delight for visitors who take the time to see it.

You should take a look at HORRABRIDGE on your way to Tavistock. The river Walkham runs right through the centre of the village and has always been the focal point of the community. There is something almost hypnotic about water flowing under a bridge and you will always find someone gazing into the bubbling water below where it overlooks the salmon leap. Here on the river you may see the occasional 'Duck Derby'.

It is not for its architectural interest that one goes to Horrabridge but to walk along the river Walkham where the variety of wildlife is quite wonderful. Kingfishers and herons are regularly to be seen. A little further downstream from 'Magpie' bridge there is a superb walk through woodlands and open glades where the Walkham and the river Tavy meet at a point known as Double Waters. When my children were young we spent many happy hours here playing Pooh Sticks! It is a splendid spot for a picnic as well.

Historically Horrabridge has a place because in the 16th century Katherine of Aragon passed through at 16 years of age, on her way to meet Henry VII and his eldest son Arthur, with whom a marriage had been arranged. She had landed at Plymouth where she was feted by the local nobility and also attended a service in St Andrews Church. The local hostelry is THE LEAPING SALMON where the food is good and the beer well kept.

Between Princetown and Tavistock there is another super hostelry, THE DARTMOOR INN at Merivale Bridge. It dates from the 17th century, with all the character that one might expect from a pub of this age. It is the sort of place that when you call in for a drink you immediately feel at home and think I would not mind staying here for a few days, and so you should for not only is it welcoming it is also beautifully situated for anyone wanting to walk on the open moor at any time of the year. In summer it is cool but in winter the pub radiates warmth. The sweeping views of the moorland are stunning and I would be quite satisfied sitting and drinking in the sight. Mark you I would also be assured of an excellent meal and possibly a bottle or so of the country wines for which The Dartmoor Inn is famous.

Sheepstor

Tavistock has its own chapter in this book so I am by passing it to go on to the many villages closeby. Towards Cornwall there is CHILSWORTHY on the Cornish border, a quiet oasis made memorable by its true country pub - something that is becoming more and more rare. Just six miles from Tavistock, THE WHITE HART INN has everything, atmosphere, comfort, wonderful views overlooking the spectacular Tamar Valley, comfortable and very reasonable bed and breakfast accommodation, and to cap it all, a charming 24 seater restaurant in which excellent West Country food is served daily. For those who want somewhere to stay, drink or eat before or after a visit to the International St Mellion Golf Course, it is ideal and only 5-10 minutes drive away. For walkers it is about four fifths of the way round the Railway walk from Gunnislake and somewhere not to be missed.

From here it would be sad not to take a look at MORWELLHAM QUAY just off the A390 going towards Gunnislake. Situated in an unspoilt valley it is the recreation of a Victorian copper port, once described as the greatest copper port in Queen Victoria's Empire. You will find people dressed in costumes of the time, a riverside tramway going underground into an ancient copper mine, last worked in 1868, woodland trails along the river banks, a 19th century farm, a fascinating museum, blacksmith's shop, coopers' and assayers. The whole adds up to a wonderful family day out and helps you to discover 1,000 years of history.

On the other side of the A390 a turning to the right will take you to GULWORTHY and one of the best restaurants with bedrooms in the whole of England. THE HORN OF PLENTY is a country house of beauty and elegance. To lunch or dine here is a gastronomic feast. Not inexpensive, it is worth every penny and for those who want to be pampered, staying a night or two could not be bettered. I lunched there a short time ago on one of the rare good Spring days that we have had, and apart from relishing the food, the staggeringly beautiful views did nothing but aid the digestion and leave a lasting impression.

Weir Quay, Bere Alston

Strictly speaking GUNNISLAKE is not part of Dartmoor and in fact is in Cornwall but it is very easy to stray over the border and certainly worth while to seek out the 17th century village inn, THE RISING SUN, whose proprietors are Martin and Philippa Finn It is a rustic hostelry in a perfect spot. You will find it just as you get through the centre of Gunnislake on the road to Calstock. The first thing that will strike you is the stunnng view of the Tamar Valley followed smartly by the realisation that the gardens are exceptional. There always seems to be something flowering and in season the array of colours is fabulous. It is a pub that suits all ages, Martin cooks delicious traditional food and every Monday there is good pub entertainment. This also occurs occasionally at weekends. Theme nights are eagerly awaited. It might be Arabian, Italian or a 60's night. Always good fun, these evenings are heavily attended.

Another first class pub in the locality is tucked away in the valley at HORSEBRIDGE, just 200 yards from the Cornish border. THE ROYAL INN AND HORSEBRIDGE BREWERY is almost abreast of the bridge, the first ever to be built linking the two counties of Devon and Cornwall and was completed in 1437 by the Monks at Tavistock. It was about fifty years later that the building which is now the pub appeared, built by the same monks, as a nunnery. It was Henry VIII after the Dissolution who gave the building to the Bedford family and they decreed it should be an inn. At that time it was named the Pack Horse but that name disappeared after Charles I visited the pub before the Civil War. His seal is still to be seen on the doorstep and so it became The Royal Inn.

Morwellham Quay

This family run pub also brews its own beer. Simon Wood, son of the proprietors is the chief brewer of the smallest brewery in the country. There are three brews normally, varying in strength and a 'Right Royal' one for high days and holidays. It is a delightful pub, full of character and characters! Food, glorious food, is the best way to describe what you will eat. Mrs Wood and her assistant, whom she calls 'Amazing Grace' enjoy cooking the sort of meals you do not get at home. You will never see a chip served here. The emphasis is on good, wholesome food and an abundance of delicious salads. Vegetarians will love it and those who have a sweet tooth will never forget 'Divine Decadence'!

Wandering across country a bit will bring you to MILTON ABBOT and so to ENDSLEIGH GARDENS, a place of beauty and learning. Here you can look at beautiful trees and shrubs in superb surroundings and enjoy choosing from the extensive range of plants. To find Endsleigh turn opposite Milton Abbot school.

Pass through sleepy Milton Abbot and after approximately one and a half miles taking a right turn for Bradford Kelly, a little further on you will come to FELLDOWNHEAD and COUNTRYMAN CIDER, the owners of which produce some of the best cider in Devon. Bob and Anne Bunker are a fascinating couple, who took on the onerous task of rescuing Countryman Cider some four years ago when it was almost defunct. For many years in the hands of the Lancaster family, Countryman Cider had enjoyed an enviable reputation but when Horace Lancaster decided to retire it was sold to people who were not as interested nor experienced and the business suffered.

It has been the sheer determination of the Bunkers as they cleared out the rotten barrels, rejuvenated the press and fought long and hard to obtain the right size and shape containers which hold exactly the measurements laid down by the E.E.C., which has brought them success. When I was there some three years ago they had just built themselves a new house in what was an old barn and planted out a new orchard, which for sometime looked like a War Graves cemetery, each tree marked with a cross and protected by a white covering. Now the little trees are sturdy.

Getting the right apples is not the easiest task either. I asked where the apples came from and was told that it is largely the generosity of people who respond to an advertisment for cider apples and subsequently turn up at Countryman Cider, some with a vanload and some with plastic bags full to bursting. Generally speaking it was not for the money that these people brought their produce but to receive some cider as their reward. In my ignorance I thought that all apples were suitable for cider-making but this is not the case; the true cider apple is very pithy.

It is not only locally that the cider is sold. Bob has opened up accounts all over Devon and Cornwall, in the Home Counties, London and the Midlands - and he is constantly increasing his contacts. With the meticulous attention to the stages of cider-making, he has achieved outstanding results.

Anne Bunker looks after the shop where you can buy the cider on draught, dry, medium or sweet, or mixed to your own taste. It comes in 5 gallon, 5 litre and 2.5 litre containers or in bottle sizes of 1 litre and 75cl. I must confess to a preference for the attractive earthenware jars or bottles rather than plastic containers. Mead can also be bought here as well as some interesting country wines and cider vinegar. If you have never cooked with Cider, talk to Anne about it. She has tried out many recipes successfully and has put the method down on paper. You can buy these recipes in the shop as well.

Have you ever heard the legend of Tavistock Abbey's famous drink? Now, when I have been writing about Countryman Cider, is probably the time to tell you. Green Devon apples have always been used for cider making and at one time the orchards of Tavistock were renowned for their cider apples. The cider produced was palatable but a trifle rough and not always sweet enough. The monks at Tavistock put this right by adding a liberal quantity of sweet white wine, but they nonetheless kept on trying to improve the cider without this additive - it had the tendency to make the monks drunk and it was certainly not conducive to the quiet, contemplative thinking obligatory to the order!

The abbot offered a prize to anyone who could discover the means of making the cider smooth without using the wine. Many solutions were offered but none was successful. One day, however, an old man limped up to the gate and told the monks that he had travelled the world and worked on various liquors, even the famous benedictine, and he was quite prepared to offer his services. The abbot offered his guest a room and food, both of which were declined and the visitor said that all he needed was an empty cask in which to rest. The monks were impressed at this total disregard for personal comfort, except one, Brother Lenoard who thought there was something strange about the visitor. He decided to keep an eye on him, and later that night he crept into the brewing room and carefully removed the cover of the cask in which the old man was sleeping. To his amazement he saw a cloven hoof protruding from under the old man's robe. Brother Leonard was horrified - the Devil had tricked his way into the abbey.

Quickly he worked out a plan and connected a hosepipe to the main vat. Taking it to the cask he attempted to drown the visitor in cider. The cider was cold and awakened the old man, who spluttering and cursing, assumed his Devilish shape, leapt from the cask amid a cloud of sulphurous fumes and disappeared.

By this time the cask was almost full of cider and so Brother Leonard rushed to turn off the supply. He was reluctant to throw away such a large quantity of cider but he realised it was probably undrinkable. He thought, however, that he should take a sip just to see and was amazed to discover that the contents were sweet and delicious to taste and lacked all the rough edginess which he and his brothers had been trying to eradicate from the brew.

From that day onwards Brother Leonard always poured all the rougher kinds of cider over burning sulphur and soon Tavistock Abbey became famous throughout the West Country for its delicious, sweet, mellow cider. Henry VIII put paid to all this at the time of the dissolution and so the secret of the sweet cider has been lost. It is said that as much as you may enjoy Devon's traditional drink, it can never match the cider once brewed at Tavistock Abbey. Wonderful story but I think you will find Countryman Cider has rediscovered the secret - try some!

The village of NORTH BRENTOR has about 300 inhabitants and stands on the edge of Dartmoor about five miles from Tavistock. Its greatest claim to fame is its astonishing church, St Michael de Rupe which stands sentinel some 1,100ft above sea level. How it got there is the subject of many a legend and the one that seems to be most popular tells of Hugh a wealthy merchant. One day his ship was sighted making her way up the English Channel returning from the Far East with a cargo of silks and spices. The Devil caught sight of the vessel and decided that he had been too long without any victims because of the vigilance of the Dartmoor people. He created a terrible storm, making sure at the same time the strength of the wind and rain put out the warning beacons on the coast, and on the top of Brennon or Beacon Tor which is now called Brentor. No matter how the skipper of the merchantman handled his ship, it was inexorably driven towards the rocky coast. Hugh the merchant was terrified and he stayed below decks praying hard for safe keeping.

Throughout the night the Devil flew over the stricken ship, screaming with glee and the thought of certain death for the crew and the passengers. Towards morning Hugh came on deck to be told that nothing more could be done by mortal hands. He at once knelt on the deck and prayed to his patron saint, St Michael vowing that if the ship were saved he would build and dedicate a church to the saint on the highest point of land he first sighted. His prayers were answered, the wind slackened and changed direction taking the ship out to sea and away from certain destruction. The Devil huffed and puffed but was impotent against the power of St Michael.

Hugh, the merchant, was a man of honour and he immediately set out to build the church on Brentor which was the first and highest point of land sighted after the storm. A lesser man might have given up when he saw the difficulties of building on such an inacessible spot, but not Hugh, he toiled unsparingly giving freely of his money and his energy until he had assembled all the required materials on top of the tor. When the last stone was deposited at the top Hugh felt quite triumphant and happily looked forward to the completeion of the church. The Devil had other ideas. He saw what Hugh was doing and was furious to think that the man who had foiled his best laid plans should be succeeding in this quest. During that night he scattered all the building materials at the foot of the tor. Shattered by the discovery Hugh was momentarily despondent but he remembered his promise and set about bringing the materials up the tor once more. Each night the Devil returned and threw them all to the bottom again until after some weeks St Michael heard about it and went to Hugh's aid. When the Devil arrived that night he found Saint Michael waiting for him. The saint hurled a huge granite boulder at the Devil who had turned to run away. He did not escape unhurt; the boulder caught him on the heel and sent him off roaring with anger as much as pain. The injury was sufficient to keep the Devil away and Hugh was able to complete his task.

BRENTOR CHURCH

When the church was dedicated it was pointed out that it was the smallest on the Moor instead of one of the most splendid as Hugh had intended. The problem lay in the fact that Hugh's huge loss of money in his tussle with the Devil had left him short of cash. It matters not, the church still stands today, dedicated to St Michael and a credit to the guts, determination and faith of Hugh the Merchant.

You will not find a shop in the village but it boasts a first class pub, THE BRENTOR INN built in 1700 for travellers especially at the turn of the century when it was a coaching inn.

At that time it was called the Herring Arms after a former landlord, Phil Herring who is reputed to haunt the inn. People come here for several reasons. It is ideal for anyone who enjoys walking this part of the moor and is brave enough to climb up to the church. It has a small dining room, excellent traditional and substantial home-cooked food plus a couple of letting rooms which are comfortable and inexpensive.

On the outskirts of the village there is ROWDEN GARDEN, a water garden supplying exotic aquatic plants, a nursery producing bedding plants and shrubs.

Coles Cottage at SOUTH BRENTOR is the headquarters of TAMAR FUELS, owned and run by Peter and Sue Heal. This friendly couple run a most efficient service for their customers, delivering coal and other solid fuels. So many people in the country still have the joy of open fires that such a service is essential and welcomed especially at houses in isolated areas. However deliveries are not only confined to rural areas, Tamar Fuels runs regular and reliable deliveries to all parts of Plymouth and West Devon.

The A386 from Tavistock to Okehampton passes through several villages of charm and interest. The two Tavys, Peter and Mary lie just up the road from the old Stannary town of Tavistock. Neither seems to suffer too much from the 20th century. These twin villages grew out of ancient settlements on either side of the River Tavy and both are blessed with a church, St Mary's and St Peter's which are a mile apart and joined by a bridle path, bridged by 'The Clam' - an old name for a bridge, I am informed. Mining provided the wealth of the two villages until the 1920's and you can still see many old workings scattered around the area. Wheal Friendship in Mary Tavy, was once the largest copper mine in the world and later produced arsenic, which was exported from Morwellham.

At one time it was all taken away by packhorse until the mine manager, John Taylor had the foresight to commission the Tavistock Canal in 1817. Wheal Betsy engine house stands out clearly as you pass by on the A386. This was part of the extensive workings of an old silver and lead mine using Cholwell Brook to provide the force for the many water-wheels. Here women worked on the surface, breaking up the ore. They were known as Bal Maidens. Bal is an old word for a mine and more frequently in use in Cornwall than Devon.

William Crossing, the famous and revered writer on Dartmoor lived in a cottage here called 'Crossing. It was here that he wrote the much loved and constantly read 'Guide to Dartmoor' and many others. He was often to be seen in the two villages gathering stories. He and his wife are buried in Mary Tavy churchyard.

WHEAL BETSY

Both villages have excellent pubs. Peter Tavy has an inn of that name that is as old as time, with low ceilings, beams and a wonderful atmosphere. Its food is renowned locally. In Mary Tavy, THE ROYAL STANDARD has stood since the 16th century. Over the centuries the building has been considerably altered but it has never lost its sense of stability. It is as welcoming inside today as it has always been and at one time provided hospitality for Royalty, hence its name. Good pub food is available every day of the week.

Mary Tavy has two other excellent establishments. THE STANNARY on the main road offers gourmet vegetarian cuisine in the beautiful surroundings of an elegant 16th century and part Victorian house. It has been showered with accolades justifiably. Many of the dishes are created from unusual and exotic ingredients, with truffles, seaweeds, edible flowers and wild berries frequently featured. The Stannary is ideal for anyone wanting creatively unique and well prepared food plus comfortable surroundings, whether on a visit for dinner or staying in one of the guest rooms. Strictly a non-smoking establishment, it is also advisable to dress smartly if you wish to dine.

Just off the A386 on the Brentor road from which you will see it signposted, is THE MOORLAND HALL HOTEL. The hotel stands in five acres of gardens and paddocks with plenty of parking space. It is a place in which to recharge your batteries and soak up the peacefulness. There are eight well appointed en-suite bedrooms two of which have four-poster beds. There is a welcoming bar and a quiet lounge where you can relax and enjoy the books and magazines left for you. The bar billiard table is fun for those who enjoy the game. The restaurant which is open to non-residents who have previously booked, is non-smoking.

The Stannary

Ask the Farrs, who own Moorland Hall, about Gibbet Hill and they will tell you that it is where celebration bonfires are lit and attracts people to take part in national events. On the unpleasant side you will also be told that this is where they used to hang criminals. The sight of the corpse, left hanging on the gibbet, was thought to be a deterrent to the would be sheep stealer or highwayman. The prisoners awaiting execution were kept in cages at the foot of the hill.

Legend says that one Lady Hill who was notorious for murdering her husbands, drives through Mary Tavy at midnight in her coach which is made out of her victims' bones and behind follows a baying black hound. Until she has picked every blade of grass from Okehampton Castle and taken it back to Fitzford in Tavistock, her spirit will not be allowed to rest. If you are looking for a good, moorland pub with an odd name, then seek out THE ELEPHANT'S NEST in the tiny hamlet of HORNDON. Here you will be delighted by its sense of days gone by and fed on very good food.

William Crossing was famous in his time for his writings and pronouncements. Today there is another William. This time Hugh Williams, a Chartered Accountant with a difference - not for him the formality of a city office. Hugh lives and runs his practice from Lower Willsworthy, a moorland farm, at Peter Tavy. He may not write about Dartmoor in the same manner as William Crossing but he is as dedicated to its survival and its fight against the intrusion of the masses. This is a man who was once accountant to the Consumers Association who publish the magazine Which,before returning to his native West Country and starting his firm in 1973. To come to his office, you find yourself crossing the farmyard amidst the usual hubbub of farming life. Reassuring for the timid who find an accountant almost as daunting as a dentist and for the hardy, experienced client, a refreshing experience in a world that seems to be entirely synthetic.

In 1987 Hugh was appointed by the Secretary of State for the Environment to serve on the Dartmoor National Park Committee. Throughout this time he has been dealing with his own clients to whom he says that accountancy, contrary to public impressions, is not about calculations. It is about people. An accountant's job is to help people make money and then advise on tax implications which concern everyone. His overriding aim is to provide a personal, helpful, prompt, encouraging and friendly service. Without exception this is what his clients will tell you has been achieved. His books on accountancy are well known but probably less well known is his personal paper on National Parks and Farming. This well researched document discusses the problem, its worsening and offers a suggested solution. It covers improving the taste of our farm products, the supporting of native breeds, using natural farming methods in the National Parks and fostering the creation of markets for National Park products. It is this document which marks him down as one of those who care very deeply about the future of Dartmoor.

Unless I had used the A-Z method of writing about these Dartmoor villages, my journey was bound to be erratic so forgive me for taking you now to the northern part of the moor before returning to what is for me the most fascinating part of this granite mass.

The village of SOURTON further north past Lydford, from Mary Tavy on the A386rises at Sourton Tor to a height of 1,447ft. It has few inhabitants but covers a large area. It has been a settlement almost since time began and from time to time bronze spearheads left by ancient tribes have been dug up. Its most interesting feature is the chiefly 15th century church with a sturdy tower, not all of which is 15th century some of the masonry comes from earlier centuries. In the chancel there is a 13th century lancet with much ancient glass. The old roofs have quaint bosses and angels. It is worth seeing if only to stand in the old churchyard and revel in the stunning view. I read somewhere that in 1870 the villagers tapped spring water and left it to freeze in stone tanks. These slabs of ice were then driven to Plymouth in a horse drawn waggonette and sold to fishmongers. Brilliant idea but no one had quite calculated the ratio of the distance to the freezing point, and the ice melted in transit!

Since the 6th century the village has treasured Sourton Cross and fought for its survival. It has now been removed and re-sited for the third time because of road developments but the cross has withstood the indignity of the uprooting each time. Another time honoured Sourton custom is that every seven years the age-old ceremony of the Beating of the Bounds takes place. Its organisation is the responsibility of the Sourton and Bridestowe Commoners. At 10am on the appointed day all the walkers and helpers gather at 'Iron Catch Gates' on the moor. The food for the day is always the traditional pasty plus sandwiches and ale. Every walker has his or her own pack and then after a short service they all move off, some on horseback, passing boundary stones marked 'S' which they strike or walk around.

Once the village inn was just that, a meeting place for locals but it had its name changed to The Highwayman some years back and is now a tourist attraction. Not the sort of pub you would want to make your local but it has to be one of the most extraordinary in decor in the whole of the country. Worth a visit just to marvel at what has been done - I will say no more, you may love it. I have a sneaking regard for it because some years ago my car had a puncture when I was virtually outside the door. The landlord could not have been kinder or more helpful; my tyre was changed, I was watered and well fed and sent on my way. I felt it to be the true spirit of inn-keeping.

BRIDESTOWE, pronounced Briddystow, is totally unspoiled and seems to have forgotten the 20th century. It lies peacefully at the junction of two streams on the western edge of Dartmoor, bypassed by the main road. It is a place of stone and slate cottages, a village school, the post office cum stores, and a 15th century parish church. For such a small place it manages to sustain two good inns, THE WHITE HART and THE ROYAL OAK, the latter a coaching inn complete with a sundial that displays the date of 1714.

The village community once consisted of tin and copper miners, quarrymen, farm, railway and peat workers as well as those who worked on the big estates. In those days few people ever left Bridestowe but now the changes are frequent and all sorts of people share in the life of this pretty place. There is a nice story told about Squire Bidlake who owned the Elizabethan Manor, Bidlake House. During the Civil War and after the Battle of Torrington, the squire escaped, pursued by Roundheads and just managed to reach his home ahead of his pursuers. He changed into a cowman's smock and walked down the drive to meet them. They stopped him and asked if he had seen the squire. The response came in broad Devonshire ' No, I bain't seen 'im but I knowed he did take an 'oss from stables and rode on 'im off to France'.

Charles I is supposed to have stayed at Great Bidlake on the 30th July 1644 and the other piece of reputed history is that the house is haunted by a previous lady of the manor.

It is natural from Bridestowe and Sourton to go on towards Okehampton,which has a chapter of its own, so we will by pass that and make for STICKLEPATH on the A382, lying on the banks of the River Taw, three and a half miles east of Okehampton. This road has been the main Exeter to Cornwall highway from the earliest times and that is how the village acquired its name. 'Stickle' means steep path and applies to the climb up the hill at the western end of the village.

It is a village of strong Wesleyan connections. John Wesley preached here in 1743 and helped develop the movement resulting in the building of the present chapel. Several Sticklepath Quakers sailed with William Penn to help found the new World colony of Friends in Pennsylvania.

Sticklepath has grown and although there are some 24 buildings listed as being of historical interest, including two 17th century thatched inns, the houses of the 20th century outnumber the old. The influx has not taken away much that is traditional including the great Sticklepath oak on which there is a preservation order, thanks to the unrelenting campaign waged by the Womens' Institute when it looked in danger of being cut down to make way for a new estate of houses.

Most people work away from the village today but in the 19th century it was a busy centre of industry with two woollen mills and a flour mill. The Cleave Mill was operated by the Pearse family in the 1800's and there is a true story told about one of the Pearse family and their industry. In 1918 Lieutenant Colonel Pearse, aide de camp to the Governor of Assam, was sent to visit the Nizam of Hyderabad. When the Colonel was introduced the Nizam said 'Pearse? I know that name. He looked through some documents and found bills for scarlet cloth bought from Pearse of Sticklepath which had been made into uniforms for the palace guards at that time. 100 years on the uniforms were still in use.

The fast flowing waters of the River Taw meant that in the 19th century six or seven water wheels were able to provide the power for mills such as Pearses and other rural industries. Among these was the foundry run by the Finch family from 1814 - 1960 who produced agricultural hand tools and tools for the tin and copper mines and china clay industry of Devon and Cornwall. At one time there were seven memers of the Finch family employed here as well as 20 local men. The arrival of mass produced tools from the Midlands killed the business and by 1960 it was bankrupt.

It looked as though this remarkable place would be lost to posterity, but along came Richard Barron, a descendant of the Finch family, and he made it his business to rescue the foundry and turn it into a Museum of Rural Industry. He was not to live long enough to achieve it, but the project was taken on by Bob Barron and his sister Marjorie, so Sticklepath, once called 'the village of water wheels' still has what can only be described as a museum of the greatest possible historical and educational value. You can see the buildings and machinery, mill leat and launder (a wooden aqueduct used to wash out debris), all restored to working order. Three great wheels drive the forges, cutting shears, grindstone and polishing wheel, and a pair of heavy tilt hammers which can be seen in motion. It is now looked after by the same people who deal with the Museum of Dartmoor Life in Okehampton, part of the North Dartmoor Museums Association.

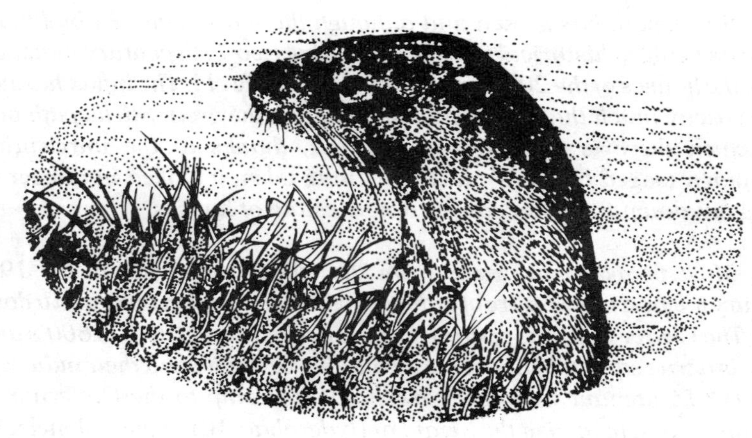

TARKA COUNTRY

SOUTH ZEAL should not be ignored. Thankfully the main A30 avoids the village and so it is a place of peace with a picturesque appearance. They still drive sheep along the main street and the sound of horses hooves is almost as familiar as the engine of a car. THE OXENHAM ARMS is the local hostelry which sits in the centre of the village. It is an old building parts of which are thought to date back to the 12th century. It is named after the Oxenham family whose home it was in the 16th century.

I was in SHEEPWASH one day and made the mistake of saying I did not think it was part of Dartmoor. I was so firmly put in my place and told about its situation and that of nine other villages who consider themselves to be part of the northern Dartmoor area, that I now find myself saying 'Welcome to northern Dartmoor'! It is lovely, a place of gently rolling hills, full of traditional Devon farmsteads, quiet villages, small towns and rivers that sparkle as they meander lazily along. Nothing is rushed here, so take your time and relish the local walks, the villages and the people. You will find that many of the villages I mention are near to or on the Tarka Trail - a long distance footpath which allows you to quietly explore the countryside as Henry Williamson described it in his classic book 'Tarka the Otter'.

TARKA COUNTRY incidentally is a name coined to identify the 500 square miles of northern Devon which gave Henry Williamson the inspiration to write Tarka the Otter. Its unspoilt countryside ranges from the wild moorland of Exmoor and Dartmoor to the tranquil river valleys between. There are 180 miles along the Tarka Trail which allows walkers to follow the travels of Tarka in a figure of eight circuit centred on Barnstaple. The southern part of Tarka Country takes in the core of northern Dartmoor including Cranmere Pool, source of five of Devon's major rivers. The route is uncharted, relying on the walker's skills at map reading and reading the landscape.

If you feel this is too much for you there is a less exacting, but nonetheless, interesting route, which follows the fringes of the moor between Okehampton and Sticklepath on the Two Museums Walk, which can be accomplished in a couple of hours. From Sticklepath the Tarka Trail continues on along country lanes and public footpaths, through the peaceful farmland bordering the upper reaches of the river Taw to Eggesford. Here it joins the train to provide a journey in comfort on the Tarka Line beside the ever widening river valley, to Barnstaple.

A bit more energetic is the cycle route from Sticklepath which follows country lanes to Hatherleigh and on to join the disused railway line at Petrockstowe, near Meeth. From Meeth, there are more than 30 miles of off-road cycling to be enjoyed - all the way to Bideford and Barnstaple, with marvellous views out across the Taw-Torridge estuary with its special bird life.

Information about walking and cycling in Tarka Country can be obtained from the Tarka Country Tourist Association, PO Box 4, Chumleigh EX187YX. Tel: 0837 83399.

From Okehampton if you continue up the A386 you will see a sign for NORTHLEW. Set on the top of a hill, the village has been built around one of the largest ancient market squares you will ever come across. The square is home to a water pump and an old cross, where it is said, the devil caught a cold and died! Its partly 12th century church is a gem. Inside is a medieval wagon style roof and a superb carved wooden screen. The eight sided village cross near the church gate dates from the 15th century. If this intriques you, you will be delighted to know that there are crosses of even earlier origin at neary EASTACOMBE and DURDON on the road to Okehampton. Walkers will enjoy Northlew as a centre which starts many walks around beautiful countryside. Particularly popular is a short, waymarked route which begins in the churchyard and offers super views of Dartmoor. It follows the top of the river valley and returns to the village along a track. It is the haunt of much wildlife including the busy squirrel and many birds.

Do you savour a really good sausage? For that if for no other reason you should go to HIGHAMPTON and to just beyond on the Hatherleigh road, where a specialist shop sells a range of scrumptious award winning sausages. I know people who travel for miles just to get this delicacy which will make you realise how indifferent most sausages are. The village is unusual and of Saxon origin. It has developed along the main road and in so doing has caused its Parish Church and rectory to become somewhat isolated on a ridge. It is worth making the effort to reach it if only for the superb views south towards Dartmoor. THE GOLDEN INN is a good hostelry with tame pheasants in the beer garden and within a few miles of trout and carp lakes which attract keen fishermen.

Another settlement since Saxon times is the village of BLACK TORRINGTON almost on the banks of the River Torridge. It has a long street leading up a hill to the fine tower of the Tudor Church of St Mary's. It is a church of interest as well as architectural beauty. In a quiet chapel, hallowed to the memory of the men who did not come back, is an oak panel of a kneeling soldier. Its 16th century Barnstaple floor tiles have been walked upon by many notable Rectors. Dick Whittington married a descendant of the earliest recorded Rector, Henry Fitzwarren, whilst a later Rector, John Russell bred the terriers which bear his name. He was known as the 'hunting parson'.

In Broad Street, THE TORRIDGE INN has cheerful owners who will tell you that 'The Welcome's Warm- The Beer's Cold'! It was from them that I discovered that the 'Black' in the village's name refers to the stones in the nearby River Torridge which turn black with iron oxides in the water.

THE TORRIDGE INN

It is probably the impressive entrance to THE GEORGE HOTEL that always stays in my mind when I think about the large village or I suppose I really should call it the market town of HATHERLEIGH. The George dates from the 15th century and was once the main coaching stage between the north and south coasts of Devon. It is our heritage at its best and this one time coaching inn still produces the atmosphere of those days.

Stand in the cobbled courtyard and you can almost hear the thundering sixes rushing mail passengers to Penzance, drawing in, the passengers thankful that they have escaped the menacing highwaymen, and looking forward to a night's rest preceded by an excellent supper and some fine ale or wine. The coaches have gone, the highwaymen are no more, but anyone staying here is still privileged. For a hundred years before the Reformation the George was a rest house and sanctuary for the monks of Tavistock and beyond. It is still a sanctuary, a place of rest, relaxation and total comfort.

Many of the cottages were originally built to house cattle, hence the broad doorways and back courtyards. Tuesday is the best day to visit Hatherleigh when the colourful market is in action. The charm of the village is enhanced by the river flowing through it and two others closeby, making it a haven for fishermen who come for a quiet and rewarding angling holiday. Surrounded by acres of moorland it has a church crowned by a shingled spire. Most of the church is well over 550 years old but I am not sure the 15th century builders would have approved of what has been done to the interior.

SHEEPWASH might seem an isolated place with not much going on but on better acquaintance you will find this is not so. During the Middle Ages this was a thriving market town and a major crossing point on the river. Now it is a small rural village where peace and quiet reigns, even in mid-Summer. It is designated as a Conservation Area and has many picturesque and traditional cob and thatch buildings with well tended gardens. The focal point of the visitor is the attractive square, complete with the original village pump but for fishermen and many others it will be THE HALF MOON INN which has fishing rights for a stretch of the River Torridge and lies at the heart of an area of Devon renowned for its excellent fishing opportunities. The bar of The Half Moon is probably the oldest remaining part of the village which was destroyed by a horrendous fire in 1742. Famous for its hospitality and uniquely homely atmosphere, the emphasis in both the bar and the dining room is on a wide range of home-cooked food. Bar snacks are available at lunchtimes, varying from cold meat salads to bowls of hot soup, or delicious home made pasties. the dining room is open every evening offering a traditional English table d'hote menu.

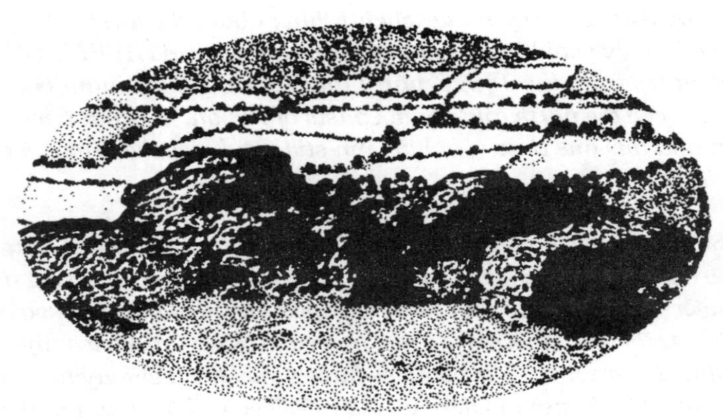

THE NORTH BOVEY VALLEY

The parish church of St Lawrence is worth visiting as much for its painted porch as you enter, as for the 'fanfare of angels' in the altar roof. To the north of the village there is a pleasant circular footpath route which takes you across Mussell Brook to Upcot Barton and back to Sheepwash. to the south of the village, downstream from the bridge, look out for the 'Sheepwash Strips'. These are a rare set of long narrow fields which have kept their oriiginal medieval outlines. The name 'Sheepwash' has the medieval form of 'Schepewast'.

What do I remember most about PETROCKSTOWE? It is a village full of surprises. To the south of the village stands The Hanging Tree where the locals will have you believe, many met their untimely end for the smallest offences. In the centre of the village is the yellow brick Chapel, and further on an unusual painted village sign depicting local scenes of horse racing, farming and railways. Once upon a time the railway line used to pass along this peaceful valley but today it forms part of the Tarka Trail. The 37 mile section from Petrockstowe north to Barnstaple and Braunton is suitable for cyclists. You can leave your car at the old station.

My favourite memory of Petrockstowe is of the church which stands high above much of the village with the war memorial at its gate. It still has a 13th century arcade and a 15th century tower. There is a Norman piscina, a Norman font with a 16th century cover, and some old heraldic glass. It is in the tower that I found what interested me most. A curious epitaph to a lady who died in 1810. It says;

She was............
But words are wanting to say what;
Think what a wife should be
And she was that.

I like MEETH for two reasons. It is described by the great Arthur Mee as 'a patch of beauty on the curve of the road, and one of the bells in the old church tower rings out, Ring me round, I'll sweetly sound.' The church stands at the end of a cobbled lime tree avenue and is mainly 15th century but part Norman. St Michael and All Angels dominates this hilltop village and within it you can inspect the parish stocks - a reminder of the days of public punishment.

My second reason is the hospitality of the 17th century BULL AND DRAGON INN. Here is innkeeping at its best. Friendly with good ale and traditional pub fare it is somewhere to make a note of. An ideal spot for those who want to enjoy farm walks, excellent fishing and cycling opportunities. You never know you might see the gentle ghost who is reported to be seen in and around the farm of Giffords Hele, a farm recorded in the Domesday book. Gifford Hele offers excellent accommodation.

MONKOKEHAMPTON is small and very quiet but nonetheless interesting. Tens of thousands of people must have seen the east window of the church. How? Why? Because it was made for the Great Exhibition in Hyde Park in 1851, before the exhibition was dismantled and the window given to the village. In its four lights are scenes from the Bible, with small figures of the Four Evangelists in the tracery above. the scenes are in medallions, showing the Shepherds at Bethlehem, the Baptism in Jordan, the Last Supper, Calvary, the Resurrection, and other sacred pictures.

The key to the church is available from the Post Office. A signed footpath at the end of the churchyard takes you on a short walk across Hole Brook and back to the village. You should take notice of the village hall which is a traditional cob and thatch reading room whose first floor cross beams can be seen on the outside of the building. This is a local building characteristic of which few examples survive. Across the road, mornings only, is a working blacksmith's forge on the wall of which is an unusual pre World War II AA sign - one of only 2 in the area. They were removed during the war to defeat any German invasion!

Much of the historic core of EXBOURNE is a Conservation Area. The local reddish soil characterises many of the rubble and cob buildings. The 15th century church has been carefully restored and is a credit to the local craftmanship. You approach it along a cobbled path and inside you will find modern oak benches carved with flowers and corn. One seat shows the Sower, and is a tribute to a rector who loved and served this church for a generation.

The fine east window has been lighting up the chancel from the day it was built and there is a 15th century screen.

JACOBSTOWE has Saxon origins and today has the Church of St James which dates back to the 15th century. The clock on the north side of the tower requires winding every day as it has since 1726. There is a pleasant walk which links Exbourne and Jacobstowe.

Between Moretonhampstead and Bovey Tracey there are seven villages which I have not yet mentioned and each has its own charm. Starting with NORTH BOVEY which is one of Dartmoor's most picturesque, unspoilt villages. It is a great favourite with artists and the many foreign visitors who come here with their cameras each year. Here a peace memorial lychgate leads to its 13th and 15th century church of St John the Baptist and inside this light and airy and much loved church are some beautifully carved bench ends, with Tudor roses created in the 16th century. The ancient RING OF BELLS is the village hostelry. An establishment not to be missed both for its atmosphere and for its role as a genuine village pub.

DUNSFORD is surrounded by wooded hills and rolling farmland going down to the pretty Teign Valley between Exeter and Moretonhampstead. Apart from being a true village with thatched cottages, its own school, a medieval church reached by steps among the thatched cottages, it has two pubs THE ROYAL OAK, one of the most comfortable pubs I have ever stayed in, where the food and drink are equal only to the hospitality. Its uninspiring exterior belies what a good hostelry it is. Very much a village 'local' but visitors are very welcome. the sort of place where there are no problems with muddy shoes or wellies. It is a starting point for many lovely walks along the River Teign. Children and dogs are welcome. The second pub at STEPS BRIDGE I have never visited but I am told by friends that it is its position that makes it special plus the excellence of the cream teas. Steps Bridge is a famous beauty spot alongside the river and is part of a nature reserve which includes Dunsford and Meadhaydown Woods. Owned by the National Trust it is run by the Devon Trust for Nature Conservation. I do not remember ever having seen so many wild daffodils as there are here in the spring.

DODDISCOMBELEIGH stands high on the hills lining the valley through which the Teign flows to the sea. While you are here you must take a look at the church because it has some of the most glorious medieval glass windows in Devon. The village also has a renowned 16th century inn, THE NOBODY INN which acquired its name reputedly because an unknown purchaser closed and locked the doors and refused hospitality to weary travellers seeking bed or refreshment. They, upon receiving no answer to their knocking, continued on their journeys in the belief that there was nobody in! It has long since outlived its reputation for its inhospitable past, and todays traveller is assured of a warm and genuine welcome. Food can be enjoyed in the bar; a favourite spot in the winter months being near the huge and imposing inglenook fireplace, under the beams that were old when Drake was busy 'singeing the King of Spain's beard. The old world ambience of the dining room provides a relaxed atmosphere in which to enjoy the good food. The restaurant offers an a la carte menu with dishes cooked from the finest, fresh, local ingredients, complemented by informal but quietly efficient service. Open from Tuesday to Saturday 7.30pm-9.30pm, it is advisable to make a reservation in advance. The bar and cellar rank with the finest in the country. The limited number of bedrooms are mostly ensuite, each with its own characteristics.

Another place of charm and interest is GREAT LEIGH FARM AND GUEST HOUSE. It is a working farm of 170 acres in which the original farm buildings and main house are set around a central courtyard, and it is these which have been transformed to provide comfortable accommodation and a dining room for guests.

The farm is above all a peaceful retreat from which, if you have the inclination, you may fly fish on the Teign, walk the nature trails, bird watch, or photograph the varied flora and fauna.

The largest barn in the complex, the old corn store, has been kept intact, and provides a magnificent setting for indoor interests such as painting, pottery and rural crafts. It also houses the snooker room, which has proved a popular after dinner haunt. Use of all the farm facilities comes free to guests.

GREAT LEIGH FARM

Great Leigh is a family run business. Colin and Angela Edwards, and Angela's sister Maria Cochrane, came together in 1992 to buy Great Leigh. Angela and Colin returned from the Mediterranean, where Colin had been pursuing his career as an aquaculturist. His knowledge of fly fishing is now put to good use in assisting guests at Great Leigh to land some of the best tasting trout in the country.

Maria Cochrane returned after eight years in Australia, where she ran a successful Sydney restaurant, to take over the kitchens. Her menu offers old favourites and some new ideas with a 'down under' flavour. Together the family strive to offer their guests the very best in comfort and hospitality. In addition to all this Great Leigh welcomes guests who would like to spend their days on the farm pursuing special interests. For these people they offer a light lunch (packed if required) and Devonshire afternoon tea free when they stay for three or more days. Special activity courses are run at Great Leigh, and day trips to the moors and other places of interest locally are also available on request.

Just off the B3193 also on the very edge of Dartmoor is BRIDFORD. Nothing very special about it but it has been a Teign valley village since the Middle Ages. Its church of St Thomas a Becket has a good congregation and when you look around you can see the loving care which is put into keeping it in the Lord's name. Bridford's remoteness and narrow steep lanes add to its charm and its views are unsurpassed. Every way you look there are panoramic scenes. Climb HELTOR ROCK, a mile to the west of the village and the vast Dartmoor wilderness is laid out before your eyes. If the day is fine and the skies clear you will see the cliffs of east Devon, their reddish colour highlighted by the sun.

Several of the towns on Dartmoor were the homes of French officers on parole during the Napoleonic wars, yet Bridford, some nine miles from Exeter became the refuge from the threat of a French invasion. Not logical, but one has to remember the difficulties of communication in those days and this underlines how remote villages like Bridford were and still are for that matter.

To the south the Benedictine Abbey of Bec, in Normandy, became the main landlord for the area that encompasses the village of CHRISTOW. The name means 'a place dedicated to Christ' but it was a settlement long before Christianity appeared. Ancient hut circles are to be seen just above the village and some prehistoric implements have been dug out dating back to the Bronze Age.

At one time this now peaceful village nestling on the bank of the river Teign, was a hive of industry after silver, lead and zinc were discovered in the area. Miners and their families flocked in to work in the mines. Wheal Frankmill employed 150 and the Wheal Exmouth, 30 men, twelve women and ten boys. Cottages were built and the village prospered. There came a time when the rich seams of mineral wealth petered out and slowly people drifted away, farming came back into its own again and peace was restored. Today it is a village the residents are proud of and gradually becoming more and more self sufficient.

High on a hill, 600 feet above sea level, overlooking the Teign valley and very close to the beauty spots of KENNICK and TOTTIFORD is the village of HENNOCK where 230 souls live a peaceful existence seldom troubled by the outside world. The bus calls once a week to take them shopping but otherwise they are comfortably self-sufficient with a good village shop, which is also the post office. The 12th century parish church of St Mary, built of granite, still has its original medieval font and one of the most beautiful old oak rood screens in Devon. Hidden behind a stone wall is the medieval thatched rectory and adjoining it is a fine tithe barn which is the village hall.

Probably the most remarkable thing about the village, and the one that wakes it up more than anything else, is LONGLANDS, once a farmstead but now a flourishing Field Study Centre, created by the Steele family. Catering for more than 40 children from schools all over the country and abroad to take up residence for a five day course. Its aims are to stimulate the childrens' minds, enhance their image of the countryside and send them home academically and physically healthier.

Time was, when annually, parties from Lancashire camped on what is now the cricket pitch in LUSTLEIGH. Escaping from the mills these northern folk would set to with a will and cut bundles of alder wood for clog making. Those days are long gone but village cricket still flourishes, at weekends you can sit and watch play surrounded by the alders, making believe that the noise and trauma of the 20th century does not exist.

Whilst villages like Manaton have remained essentially Dartmoor, Lustleigh to the east has changed completley in the last two decades.It still stands on the hillside looking down on the river, which at Horsham Steps can be heard and not seen, flowing under granite boulders. There was a time when this rural community lived simply in the beautiful valley of the Wrey. They gained their livelihood from small holdings and cultivating productive vegetable gardens, seldom venturing away. A journey to Exeter was a once in a lifetime experience. Nowadays the 13th-century church still stands. Look out for the mischievous carving of the small heads on top of the screen which was erected in Tudor times. The craftsmen obviously had likes and dislikes; all the heads facing the chancel have a secret grin on their faces and those towards the nave, a scowl.

There is no longer a railway, village school or local bobby. the doctor holds a surgery twice a week and the children are taken by mini bus to school in Bovey. Once where there were cider orchards, a few stunted trees remain; it is more economical for the cider makers to import apples.

What Lustleigh does have is THE CLEAVE, a 15th century inn in the heart of the village. There is a vast inglenook fireplace in the front bar, and in the dining room the huge granite walls are exposed. Cleave means valley and walks along it to explore the tors above the village are very popular. Many people just enjoy the delightful garden and relax with a drink as they look out on the old church and the village green.

TRUSHAM gives the impression of being remote but it is the narrow, leafy lanes which makes the approach feel inaccessible. Its houses are set into a steep hillside which leads up to the little, mostly 13th and 15th century church which treasures a Norman font and part of a Norman pillar piscina. At the bottom of the hill is the ancient CRIDFORD INN standing by a little stream. It is a friendly establishment and the locals are delighted to see visitors. A pair of ancient alms houses still stand at the top of the village proudly displaying their old biblical text on the front wall. The dwellings on this site were originally donated by John Stooke a 15th century philanthropist. You will see a 17th century monument to him and his wife in the church. Don't be amazed or alarmed if your eyes see llamas and Barbary sheep roaming the hillside - you will not have had too many beers at The Cridford! In Trusham efforts are being made to acclimatise these animals with the goal being to increase the size of the flocks and produce weavable yarn from the special wool of their coats.

Returning to the B3212, the road that crosses Dartmoor from Tavistock to Exeter, I am once more in an area that I have known and loved all my life. You drive through the most spectacular moorland. As the road dips and winds, you will find yourself revelling in the constantly changing moods and colours.

There are places where you can pull in, abandon your car and take off for a brisk walk. Along this road, too, you will see the medieval Vitifer Tin Mines and not much further on the WARREN INN, which stands at the highest point on Dartmoor. It is a great pub. There is always a roaring fire in the vast fireplace which until recently had been fuelled with peat and had not been allowed to go out for 100 years.

It is a lonely spot and I sometimes wonder how the landlord manages to remain constantly cheerful when there are days up here which are so cold, damp and dreary that no-one in their right minds would want to be in residence. I have been there a time or two when the weather has been appalling, and his welcome has always been friendly and reassuring. You can get a good meal or a bar snack, and when the weather is right there is no more spectacular view on Dartmoor.

There is the legendary story of one traveller stranded here who was given shelter providing he did not mind being put in the room where they had 'salted down feyther'. The traveller could not have cared less. He was inside a warm inn and food, drink and a bed was on offer. The room was small, bare, spotlessly clean with a single bed and a large oak chest. Thankfully he undressed by the light of a small candle and fell into bed. He slept soundly and was awakened by the sunlight pouring into the room. He sat up in bed and looked round to see if he could unravel the mystery of 'salted down feyther'. He thought it might be some kind of food but when curiosity got the better of him he opened the oak chest, and there was the body of a very old man in a white shroud. He turned and fled downstairs in terror only to find the innkeeper and his wife sitting down to breakfast. The innkeeper was shocked to see how upset his guest was, but when the man blurted out the story, he laughed and said. 'Don't you worry about that sir, the wife's father died almost two weeks ago, and the weather hasn't allowed us to take him for burial. That is why we salted down feyther!' In fact the traveller had come across a custom that was not uncommon. It was a means of preserving a body until such time as the weather lifted and made the journey to Lydford for burial possible.

As you drive across this road towards Postbridge keep a look out for Bennet's Cross, a granite edifice probably of the 14th century. If you are wondering who Mr Bennet was, the answer is that he probably was not! The most likely reason for the name is the corruption of benedict and it is likely that it was the work of one of the monks from a local monastery. It is certainly a waymark and it is one of three that you can find on this road,

POSTBRIDGE will halt you in your tracks with its famous bridge crossing the East Dart river where water jostles for position as it hits the colossal loose stones.

The bridge with its trackway, is probably as old as anything you will see in this county. It stands 1,400 feet above sea level, so you can imagine how wonderful the views are, especially if you climb LAUGHTER TOR, three miles away. All around are prehistoric remains and more fragments of the Stone Age than anywhere else on Dartmoor.

If you are in search of a riding holiday - and what better way to see Dartmoor? - then a sojourn at THE EAST DART HOTEL is for you. You can either take your own horse or allow the owners, to organize your mount. The hotel is the home of four packs of foxhounds and two hunts, so the busy bars and restaurant are magnets for those loving this sport. The stories told get more and more graphic as the convivial evening draws to a close.

On the road between Postbridge and Two Bridges there is a gate a few yards beyond Parson's Cottage, which lets you into the enclosure in which CROCKEN TOR stands. Do note that there is very limited parking here. It is quite an easy climb to the summit and an important place. For hundreds of years up to the 18th century, the Stannary Parliament met here. There were 96 members who ran the Stannaries under the command of their Lord Warden. Their job was to make the rules for the tin mining industry in Devon. It seems an odd place to meet but it was chosen because it was the most central point on Dartmoor.

TWO BRIDGES is both beautiful and has THE CHERRYBROOK HOTEL, owned and run by Andy and Margaret Duncan who since they acquired it have continued to cement their love affair with Dartmoor, and in their enthusiasm are ideal people to run such an establishment. There is nothing pretentious about The Cherrybrook which was once an old farmhouse and now with a little careful incorporation of outbuildings is comfortable, offering good accommodation, good food and good company to all who stay here, and for those non-residents who call in for a meal or for an afternoon cream tea. Its situation makes it ideal for anyone who wants to walk or explore. The Duncans told me that when they started they had no idea what to expect in this, their first venture into hotel keeping. Perhaps it is because of their naivety that they have become so successful and regularly welcome the return of guests who have become friends. Every day they learn something new about the moor and willingly pass on their knowledge to their visitors.

CHERRYBROOK HOTEL

The Cherrybrook is easily accessible but stands in some isolation and I was not surprised when Andy told me he reckoned he had seen the wild, large black puma that has stalked the moor for years. He came almost face to face with it one dark night when all he could see were luminous eyes, set in a dark face, too far apart to belong to a domestic animal. In the morning, large paw marks confirmed his belief that this was no house cat.

He reminded me also of the spectre of the 'Hairy Hand' that haunts the road between Postbridge and Two Bridges. It has put in an appearance in recent years. Even the vicar saw it and felt it - it caused him to fall off his bike! This is a fairly modern legend that seems to have started some time during the last century. It occurs only between Postbridge and Two Bridges near the southern end of the Bellever Forest where a number of incidents of coaches and horses running off the road for no apparent reason set the story going. The coachmen, when questioned, insisted that a pair of disembodied hairy hands seized the reins from them and simply drove the coach off the road. The motor car fared no better in later years. Here we are told the steering wheel was seized in a grip of steel, leaving the driver no chance to keep the car on the road. Motor cycles and even the vicar's bike have also been attacked. One specific claim just after World War II is said to have happened at a caravan parked for the night. A husband and wife were aboard. Husband had fallen asleep but the wife was writing postcards to her family and friends. Suddenly she felt something cold, eerie and ominous. Turning round she was stunned to see two hairy hands appearing through the window of the caravan. In spite of her terror she made the sign of the cross and the hands disappeared.

At DARTMEET where the east and west rivers join is PIXIELAND. I doubt if anywhere, except in Sally Satterley's garden will you ever see such a gathering of Pixies, Toadstools, Wishing Wells or Concrete Garden Ornaments, most of them made on the premises. It is worth stopping just to be amazed even if you do not believe in or like the Dartmoor Pixie. Pixieland does sell also Sheep and Goatskin Rugs, Sheepskin Hats, Mitts and Moccasins, leather Handbags, Bone China and Pottery Gifts as well as Sweatshirts and Copper Bracelets.

Past Dartmeet and on to POUNDSGATE a place to stop for and enjoy a lovely pub THE TAVISTOCK INN which is well over 700 years old. It is full of character and is renowned for its floral displays and beautiful award winning gardens. if it has any drawbacks it is the walk to the loos which can be quite chillsome in winter! There are several legendary stories about this pub. One especially tells of one of the regular drinkers at the bar who was known as 'The Snail'. He was always the butt of one of his fellow drinkers. Then one night for no apparent reason, rudeness changed to excessive politeness. He even said good night to his victim, something he had never done before. During that same night 'The Snail' died. Shock perhaps? Anyway when it was discovered he only had a few pence to his name, the regulars clubbed together and paid for a respectable funeral for 'The Snail'.

Poundsgate has some splendid walks, either short or long. one can wander along the lanes and paths towards Spitchwock and the River Dart or explore the tors to the west. If you choose to follow Dr Blackall's Drive between Mel Tor and Aish Tor, you will find the views stunning over the Dart Gorge.

On to WIDECOMBE IN THE MOOR known most of all for its famous song 'Widecombe Fair' with Old Uncle Tom Cobley and all, and for its annual fair which attracts thousands of people all intent on enjoyment. That is no bad thing but sometimes it seems to me that the overwhelming commercialism now so much a part of the Fair, takes over and the pageant of yesteryear is forgotten. You will find the green entirely devoted to stalls and fairground activities whereas in the 500 odd years that the fair has dominated the annual calendar, folk would come from miles around to see jousting, to watch the archers shooting their arrows at targets on the green. I have no doubt that Old Uncle Tom Cobley would have been one of them. Strange isn't it that this famous man was not even born, nor lived in the village! Some will tell you that he and his grey mare never even got to Widecombe! For all that an outing to Widecombe Fair is an experience which many people would never miss. I prefer the village when it is quieter and one can appreciate that from here one can see one of the best Dartmoor skylines with huge boulders and outcrops of bare rock all round.

Life is never flat here, it is very much amid the ups and downs of Dartmoor with Hameldon Ridge on one side and the Tors of Honeybag, Bell and Clinkwell on the other. Cottages huddle alongside the 15th century church which is a dignified and lofty place, known as the cathedral of the moor. It has a quaint group of old carvings and paintings. Two large ones are of Moses and Aaron and another shows Abraham offering up Isaac. The tinners helped build this church, both with their money and their time. On one of the roof bosses they left their symbol of three rabbits, each with an ear joined at the top to form a triangle. The impressive 135ft tower was nearly the church's downfall when it was struck by lightning during a service in 1638, injuring a number of the congregation.

You will hear many a legend of how the Devil had galloped through the sky on his steed followed by his whist hounds, then clung onto the tower to rest momentarily, and once refreshed, knocked it down with one careless swoop of his hand. Others tell of a story that starts in the inn at Poundsgate when the usual Sunday afternoon drinkers were disturbed by the sound of horses hooves approaching. The rider entered the bar and immediately there was an uncomfortable silence.

There was something evil about the man. He demanded a flagon of cider which he took from the shaking hands of the landlady, threw her two coins, drank it all at one gulp and was off. The landlady was sure she had served the Devil. She was right and he had just ridden on to Widecombe, where he tethered his horse to a pinnacle of the church tower. He took a look inside the church and saw a young boy asleep. This was just what he wanted for anyone sleeping in a church during a service became the property of the Devil. He snatched him and flew with him off to the pinnacle where his horse waited. As he rode off in haste he broke off the pinnacle and the startled congregation gazed aloft to see stones come crashing down. Many were hurt but no one killed, equally no one ever saw the young boy again.

Meanwhile back in the inn, the customers heard approaching hooves once more, from the direction of Widecombe and sounding just like thunder. No one looked out of the window to see who it was but it was suggested that the landlady check the money she had received from the stranger. There was no money, just two withered leaves. The oldest man in the inn shook his head and said 'Twas a good thing the pixies changed that money. They knew it were evil and so to save ee from the Devil they left the leaves. Better to 'ave leaves from the trees than evil money.'

Within this parish lies a great deal of history, medieval granite posts, crosses to mark church paths, and large boulders marked with crosses where coffins were rested on their way to the church. Another boulder with a hollow in its top is where manorial dues were paid. There are Mould stones left by tinners, granite troughs and quern wheels, also a wayside stone marked '1 MOIL' as a boundary from the days of the Napoleonic War showing prisoners the limits of their parole. To take a glass of ale in THE RUGGLESTONE INN is another experience not to be missed. It looks more like a cottage as it was originally built, than a hostelry. It was first licensed in 1850, the landlord was a farmer and stonemason. What is odd about it? It has no bar; you order your drinks in a narrow taproom which opens on to a passage, and then you take your drink to what I suppose would have been the front parlour. Nothing has been done to modernise it, apart from the installation of electricity in the 1960s - and therein lies its charm.

BUCKLAND-IN-THE MOOR is a different kettle of fish. Standing high on Buckland Beacon with the Ten Commandments carved in the stone beneath your feet, you are 1,280 feet above the sea, looking out as far as the Devon coast at Teignmouth and Torquay. Below is HOLNE where Charles Kingsley was born.

What a beautiful hamlet Buckland is, with some of the loveliest thatched cottages I have ever seen. On a hill stands the small 15th-century church with carved bosses in the porch and old tiles under the tower. The 15th-century screen is a gem with painted panels and a red and gold frieze. On one side are paintings of the Annunciation, the Wise Men and saints, and on the other some odd grey figures.

When you look up at the clock you will see that it does not have numerals. In their place are the words, 'My Dear Mother', and its bells chime out 'All things bright and beautiful'. There is no official explanation for this curiosity but legend has it that it was placed there by a man in memory of his mother. This remarkable lady, when told the news that her son had been lost at sea, refused to believe it. Every night she lit a candle and placed it in the window to guide him home. Her faith was rewarded; he did return. When she died this is how he repaid her faith.

The Perryman family have farmed at Southbrook, close to Buckland, for 40 years, surrounded by incomparable beauty. One hundred years ago the farm had the unusual distinction of having a combined out-building which dealt with everything from stabling to threshing and meant that the farmer and his men could work under cover. When this barn block fell into disrepair a decision had to be made to determine its future. There was a possibility that planning permission could have been obtained to turn it into cottages, but David and Angela Perryman felt they wanted to give something back to the community, and decided to turn the buildings into a Craft Centre. This happened three years ago and now the old buildings have a new lease of life. Downstairs is a shop selling all sorts of Devon Crafts. Alongside it is a pleasant restaurant where once the horse was harnessed to the wheel that operated the thresher.

The old stone walls have not been covered and you sit at rustic tables enjoying the good home-cooked food. Stew and dumplings never tastes better than when it is served here on Sunday at lunchtimes. As you wander round the building you will find various craftspeople at work. Take your time in looking round this centre, which is at the heart of this working stock farm, but most of all stop at the head of the stairs where there are some benches. Sit yourselves down and take a look at the view from the wide window. It is breathtaking and stretches for miles. There is no charge for walking around but I will be amazed if you are not tempted to put your hand in your pocket to buy something or at least stay awhile and have tea.

BUCKLAND-IN-THE-MOOR

The little village of HOLNE has only 300 inhabitants and has no great claim to fame but how charming it is. I like coming to it best by the road over the moor from Tavistock through Hexworthy but only in the summer; the winter tends to bring down Dartmoor fog. However the all year road from the A38 at Ashburton is beautiful in its own right, and leads you up past the entrance to the Dartmoor Country Park, over the bridge and then just before you come to the village you will see a turning to your right marked HOLNE CHASE HOTEL taking you up a drive that runs between tall trees, which are a playground for grey squirrels who dance across the driveway right in front of you, with a complete lack of regard for their safety. You are asked politely not to exceed 5mph, so perhaps the squirrels understand this.

The house at the end of the drive stands, as it has for many a long year, looking out over a vast lawn which has been the carpet for many a happy cricket match, and beyond to trees and the hills. It is a gracious house and a happy one; something one senses the moment you enter the door. Totally informal, both you, your children, your dogs and your wellies will be welcomed by one member of the Bromage family or another. The family has been here since 1972 and most of the people who come to stay from all over the world, are old friends.

The dining room looks out over the wonderful view to the tors, beyond the trees and rocks provide an ever changing colour against the sky. The food is superb. It is the sort of hotel into which one can drop for afternoon tea and feel totally at ease. Many companies use Holne Chase quite regularly for their business meetings. Something I fully understand. The facilities are right and the peaceful, out of this world atmosphere has to be conducive to clear headed thinking.

I cannot imagine anyone who would find it difficult to occupy their time whilst staying at Holne Chase, but just in case you are a keen fisherman let me tell you that the River Dart, with its tributaries, can provide some wonderful sport for salmon peel (sea trout) and brown trout. It is a spate river, so water conditions are important. The hotel has a mile of water, single bank, fly only. The season is March to September and for hotel residents there is no charge, but you must have your own equipment. Fishing is also available on Duchy of Cornwall water at a nominal charge. All fishermen must have a National Rivers Authority Licence however, which may be purchased at the hotel.

If you want to ride, Holne Chase has some of the best stables on Dartmoor within less than a half hour's drive. If you are a beginner do not despair, tuition is available. Foxhunting can usually be arranged in season.

Holne Chase has a number of short holidays based on exploring Dartmoor which are available between November and March. One of the nearby stables is LITTLECOMBE RIDING CENTRE between Holne and Scorriton, four and a half miles from Ashburton. Here experienced riders are welcome as well as novices. The stable has fit, quality horses from 15 hands. Competitive long distance riding over Dartmoor is on the menu, and Livery is available. To ride out for a full day, even if you are a novice, is a wonderful experience, especially when you are in such capable and friendly hands.

Holne has an old church which was mentioned in the 13th century and there would have been a settlement here much earlier, as tin and copper were 'streamed' hereabouts. Perhaps THE CHURCH HOUSE INN beside the church provided food and shelter for travellers who would have come along the packhorse tracks. The present inn is also ancient, and was built much at the same time as the 13th century church was enlarged, but it still dispenses friendly hospitality and good food. THE BADGERS HOLT tearooms are a popular stopping place for many visitors including a number of coach parties. I am told the Cream Teas are very special.

Hembury Castle is an Iron Age fort which has been looked after by the National Trust's careful and partial restoration. Holne Moor has interesting hut-circles, some of which have been excavated.

HAYTOR must rank as one of the most popular places on Dartmoor. The conservationists shake their heads over the increasing number of what has been described as cavalry charges over regular routes. The farmer out for a ride or two or three riders enjoying the grandeur of the moor is one thing but the increasing number of pony trekkers results in erosion and can be seen particularly on Haytor Down where, day after day, during the better months of the year, there is a constant stream of riders. I am not sure what one does about it. Who are we to stop their pleasure but equally we must save the beauty of Dartmoor for future generations.

I love standing high up on Haytor; you feel as if you control the world. Arthur Mee described it by saying 'Steps have been cut to help us to climb the high rocks stranded like a mammoth whale on this high plateau, gaunt against the skyline', or 100 feet higher RIPPON TOR which stands at 1600 feet. From here you gaze down on Teignbridge - a South Devon district of rolling farmland, estuaries, woods and heathlands. It stretches as far away as the red cliffs and sandy beaches of Teignmouth and Dawlish.

If you would like to go on one of the Teignbridge Walks which include samples of Devon's countryside at its best, or an earthwalk at Decoy Country Park (Newton Abbot), explore a leafy combe or old parkland with sea views at Teignmouth or take the children beachcombing or bird watching at Dawlish Warren Nature Reserve, then call at Dawlish T.I.C or contact the Head Ranger on 0626 61101, extension 2742.

THE TEMPLER WAY is a footpath of great historic interest, crossing a variety of landscapes from the moorland to the sea. It follows roughly the line of a 19th century tramway and canal which linked Haytor granite quarries to the Teign Estuary. From Haytor Down, you can follow the Templer Way for 15 miles, down first to Devon County Council's popular lakeside country park at Stover and on, finally to the Teign estuary shore and sea at Shaldon. Across the Becka Valley from Haytor are two popular climbs, GREATOR and HOUNDTOR, between which lies the medieval village.

There is a guided walks programme for a number of walks, many starting from Haytor car park. Ring 0626 61101, extension 2742 for more information or collect it from the Tourist Information Centres. You will find all the T.I.C's listed at the back of this book.

Haytor Vale is blessed with an excellent pub, the 18th century coaching inn, THE ROCK INN, where roaring fires are welcoming in winter and friendly hospitality with good food is available throughout the year. Here too are ten comfortable bedrooms, most of which are ensuite.The inn is said to be haunted by a 200 year old ghost named Belinda. This girl was a serving maid in the inn who had an affair with one of the coachmen. His wife was so infuriated when she found out that she beat Belinda to death on the stairs. Recent history tells us that when Lady Thatcher stayed there whilst she was Prime Minister, one of her Special Branch men was disturbed by this lifelike apparition and thinking it was an intruder, shot it. Imagine his explaining this to his none too gullible colleagues; all that remained was a hole in the wall of the inn!

A gentle warning. This tends to be an adult pub and whilst children are welcome they are not encouraged! Walkers too should take care to leave muddy wellies or walking shoes and macs etc in the foyer. Inside the beautiful furnishing is not designed for heavy wear.

If you want to stay in an exceptional small hotel then THE BEL ALP HOUSE is the answer. Once it was owned by the formidable millionairess, Dame Violet Wills, a lady who had an eye for beauty, which she put to very good use when she significantly altered this Edwardian country mansion. It is a house of large airy rooms, beautiful arches and a wonderful atmosphere. Since 1983 it has been the home of Roger and Sarah Curnock and their family, who welcome guests into this lovely house which they have furnished, elegantly and comfortably, with family antiques, paintings and an abundance of house plants. There is a quiet restfulness in all the rooms and most of them have stunning views, across the rolling fields and woodlands to the sea.

No guest ever arrives at Bel Alp without being greeted personally by at least one member of the family, who somehow always manages to remember your name. Sarah Curnock's mouth-watering cooking is something else that would always draw me back to Bel Alp. Each evening she cooks a different, carefully planned, five course dinner, with one or two alternative choices. It is no good asking her the day before what she will produce. she may have some thoughts on it but it will all depend on what is available when she shops.

Sarah looks upon her task as though she is cooking for a private dinner party for somewhere around 16 people every day. She keeps a comprehensive reference of every meal and who the guests were, so that next time they come she can ensure they do not get the same menu.

Bel Alp nestles into the hillside, 900feet up, on the south-eastern edge of Dartmoor. On a sunny day there are many perfect places in the garden to snooze away an hour, or sit and drink in the sheer beauty around you. When I was there thunderous rain was teeming down but it did not detract from the breathtaking views, merely giving them another dimension.

Not the easiest place to find, I suggest that the best way is to turn off the A38 dual carriageway onto the A382 to Bovey Tracey. From there take the B3387, signed Haytor and Widecombe. Half a mile on, fork left and go straight over one crossroads. After one and a half miles, cross a cattle grid onto the moor. Another five hundred yards fork left into the hotel drive.

From the stunning, awesome tors of Dartmoor through the leafy road that takes one almost into Bovey Tracey, makes quite a change of scenery, and when you turn off the road into PARKE RARE BREEDS FARM with its soft, undulating fields, it is a different world. The car park is set at the end of quite a long drive. You are in for quite a walk, so strong and comfortable shoes are a necessity.

Parke is run by the Rare Breed Survival Trust, which was formed in 1973 to prevent any further extinction of mainly British farm livestock. Many of the breeds that you will see are very rare indeed and I realised that if it were not for the work of this Trust, and others like it, so much of our heritage might disappear. Some of the animals can be traced back to prehistoric times. It is educational, rewarding and marvellous for children, who will revel in being allowed to handle some of the animals at the specially designed Pets Corner.

The little village of ILSINGTON is still within reach of Haytor, whose granite made London Bridge. The cottages snuggle under deep thatch and the spacious cross-shaped church is mainly of the 14th and 15th centuries. Perhaps not a village one would visit regularly but for those who have discovered THE ILSINGTON COUNTRY HOUSE HOTEL, once having been you will surely return. It is a gracious building in a tranquil moorland setting with its own extensive gardens. It is only a few minutes away from the A38 and a short distance from the South Devon coast.

The hotel is personally managed by the resident proprietor and his friendly dedicated staff. You can be assured of a high standard of service, delicious food in the candlelit dining room and warm, inviting hospitality in the lounge and cosy bar which also serves Devonshire cream teas. This is more than just a very good hotel. Resident guests enjoy full use of the leisure facilities which include an indoor heated pool, sauna, spa, steam room, fully equipped gymnasium, the all weather tennis courts and the bowling green. The highly trained staff are available for fitness assessments, beauty treatments and individually designed exercise programmes.

For those looking for somewhere for a conference, a seminar or any type of meeting or function, The Ilsington Country House Hotel, offers a complete service, and with it comes the same professionalism that is apparent in every department of this delightful hotel.

The mention of Cream Teas reminds me of yet another Dartmoor Legend, this time a love story. Dartmoor was once the home of giants and one in particular settled on DINGER TOR. Giant Blunderbus was his name and as was the custom among giants, he had four wives. His favourite was Jennie who was young and beautiful, kind and loving but somehow she had never been taught to cook.

Blunderbus loved her dearly and was always ready to sit and talk to her and frequently brought her presents. The other three wives, none as pretty or as good tempered as Jennie, were very jealous and treated her abominably, finding her all the hardest and dirtiest of jobs - a bit like Cinderella. Nonetheless Jennie was always cheerful and only sad when her beloved Blunderbus was missing. These three harpys were determined to force Blunderbus to get rid of Jennie. They nagged him to death, fed him with burnt food, refused to wash his clothes and eventually he gave in and promised to get rid of Jennie. The women were triumphant but Blunderbus was not prepared to let her go entirely, and he installed her in a cave on the Cornish Cliffs where he could visit her secretly, but they were both miserable whenever they had to part.

One day Jennie was alone in her cave and feeling very depressed when she heard voices on the rocks below. She crept to the front of the cave and looked out making sure not to be seen. Beneath her were a group of fierce looking men who were plotting to wreck a ship - they were Cornish wreckers. Jennie was terrified not only for herself but at the thought of the sailors aboard the ship who might well lose their lives. She had to do something. That night she saw the wreckers leading a donkey with a lantern attached to his saddle, forwards and backwards along the cliff top. This was an old wreckers trick which made ships think that there is another ship and plenty of deep water inshore. Jennie saw the ship turn and head towards the rocks. The only thing she could think of doing was setting fire to a heap of brushwood and driftwood which she hastily piled together. The ship saw the flames and the Captain realised the danger. He ordered his men to drop anchor and sent a boat ashore to investigate. The sailors landed only just in time because the infuriated wreckers were hunting for Jennie in order to kill her. However they themselves were overtaken by the sailors and killed without mercy.

The Captain of the ship wanted to do something very special for Jennie. She was just happy to have someone to talk to and so she told him all her troubles, told him about her giant, the other three wives who had made her life such a misery and above all how she wanted to be able to cook for her Blunderbus.

In the eyes of the ship's Captain, Blunderbus was not such a great man, for if he had been he would not have allowed his other three wives to drive Jennie out. However it was clear to him that unless Jennie could be reunited with her giant she would probably die of a broken heart. 'My dear,' he said. 'How would it be if I gave you a recipe for the most wonderful food you will ever taste and at the same time also teach you to make it. I promise that once Blunderbus has feasted on it he will never leave you again.'

The recipe was for clotted cream and on Blunderbus's next visit Jennie fed him some of this delicacy. The giant's praise for her food made Jenny very happy and even more so when he insisted that she went back with him to Dinger Tor.

The other wives were none too pleased but when they had tasted the cream, they all clamoured to know how to make it. Jenny was magnanimous enough to show them and eventually the fame of this clotted cream spread through Devon. Jenny and her Blunderbus lived happily ever after. Devon is famous for its Cream Teas so when next you sit down to enjoy one, remember you have Jenny to thank for the rich, clotted cream.

Returning towards Plymouth there are three villages bordering on the edge of the moor and not too far from the sea. Strictly speaking ERMINGTON, I believe, should be in the South Hams. In fact it has great difficulty today knowing quite where it belongs because of its proximity to the ever encroaching boundaries of Plymouth. The village is roughly three miles outside Dartmoor National Park and separated from it by a major trunk road. It is surrounded by beautiful, soft rolling countryside. There are a rich assortment of old buildings, and towards its northern end a well preserved ex-water mill now houses THE MILL LEAT TROUT FARM AND CRAFT CENTRE. The Trout Farm in the capable hands of Christopher Trant, takes its name from the Leat, or watercourse, that runs down to the River Erme. The mill ceased to be operational some years back and even the grinding stones have been removed but the old building flourishes. It is the home of several enterprising businesses which have grouped themselves round the Trout Farm.

People come from quite a wide catchment area to catch and collect their trout. beautiful, plump fish that are delicious to eat. Youngsters come here and are taught how to catch a fish and once they get the hang of it they come back time and time again, bringing their parents with them of course. Much of the work is done for catering establishment who ring up and order daily. It is Christopher who has to go out rain or shine and catch the fish ready for the customer to collect or have delivered.

Over the years trout has not only become more popular with the general public but the price has come down to acceptable levels. Pound for pound it is probably as cheap as any fish in the market today. Running this farm takes a lot of skill and knowledge. It looks simple enough when you stand on the little wooden bridge looking down at the fish pens, but for Christopher Trant to feel he was sufficiently well informed to cope, it meant a post graduate course on Fresh Water Biology. Mill Leat is open all the year round but during the winter it is open from 9-5pm for five and a half days and in the summer everday from 9-5.30pm. It is an enjoyable outing.

The crooked spire of the 13th century church tower looks down on the village and the delighful wooded valley of the River Erme. Its crookedness is the most arresting feature of the village because it is quite literally bent. Legend has it that in the 14th century a Miss Bulteel was married before the altar of this already ancient church. Such was her beauty that the spire was overawed and bowed to her as she entered the portals. It was so old it was never able to straighten itself again. The spire you see today, still crooked, was rebuilt in 1850 after the original was badly damaged by lightning. The villagers who raised the money for the new spire, cherished the earlier one so much that they had it rebuilt in the bowing position.

Inside the church there is much that demands attention but for me the most impressive feature is the carved work, old and new. Violet Pinwill is responsible for the new. This talented lady was the daughter of the rector who preached here for nearly half a century. Every corner of the building has something of beauty that is attributable to Violet. A charming oak panel in the sanctuary has two carved and coloured scenes showing the church as it looked when her father first came to it. Her work is also to be seen on the carved bench-ends, the delicately pinnacled cover of the old font. To crown her work she restored the beams and bosses of the superb chancel roof. She will be long remebered too for the glory of her work.

UGBOROUGH is another edge-of-the Moor village but never feels quite like a moorland village to me. It has too much closeness to the sea verified by the robust sea breezes which blow through it. It is a pleasant place sitting in a sheltered bowl, surrounded by farmland, lush fields and small copses. It has a busy village life, two good pubs THE SHIP and THE ANCHOR bringing home even further Ugborough's connections with the sea. Its ancient church is remarkable for its length - 131 feet from end to end. The ornate list of vicars is unusual inasmuch as it not only records their names but those of the Kings and Queens of the same dates and great events of history.

The hidden village of CORNWOOD is truly on the Moor. It has a small open square, a good pub and a church with a squat tower and weathered stonework. It was at the font of St Michael and All Angels that the father of Sir Walter Raleigh would have been baptised. The church is not particularly easy to find but worth seeking out.

The pub, THE CORNWOOD INN is welcoming if not oustanding apart from the fact that it is a 'Letter Box' site. The walks in the area are full of variety. To the north-west lie, Rook gate, Shell Top and Lee Moore (owned by the National Trust). To the north-east, tracks and roads lead to Stalldown barrow and the Two Moors Way while to the south-east are lanes and farm paths leading to Hanger Down.

And so back to Plymouth in the knowledge that Dartmoor with all its awesome majesty is only a short way away.

DEVONSHIRE CLOTTED CREAM

Put fresh full cream milk in a large bowl and leave to stand for approximately 12 hours in summer (24 hours in winter). Stand the bowl over a pan of water and heat slowly, being careful not to boil the water. Leave until thick crust has formed over the surface of the milk. Stand it in a cool place until the following day, then carefully skim the scalded cream from the top of the milk.

In this day and age when young scholars seem to be less and less interested in the past glories of England, I still find it hard to believe that anyone cannot be stirred by the history of the greatest sailor since the world began, Sir Francis Drake. Everytime I come to Tavistock I am thrilled to be where this great man was born at Crowndale Farm, and who was probably baptised in the beautiful parish church of St Eustachius. Tavistock is one of the most interesting and alive Stannary towns in the whole of Devon and Cornwall. A town where Tavistockonians - those who have been here forever - have welcomed the outsiders who have come to make it their home, and live in the many new estates which have grown up on the outskirts.

Long before Drake, Tavistock was already a busy place. It is one of the oldest parts of Devon to be inhabited. Prehistoric settlers were here and it is first recorded in history about a hundred years before the arrival of William the Conqueror. The story starts with the building of the Abbey, founded by Ordgar, whose daughter had been maried to King Edgar. It was not a peaceful time and the first abbey was destroyed by the Danes, but was soon to be rebuilt by Ordulph, the son of Ordgar. The religious life was rich and had great influence over the town. It was during this time that Tavistock received a charter and became a market town. The Abbey ruled the town until Henry VIII broke up the monasteries throughout the country, and gave the estates to his friends. Tavistock Abbey was given to John Russell who became the first Earl of Bedford. His family have had much to do with the prosperity of the town.

Drake never knew, in the fickle court of his Queen, Elizabeth I, whether he was to be treated as a pirate or a heaven-sent saviour of the realm. It is difficult for us to understand a time when our island was almost a prison. We were at the mercy of the Spaniards and under the tyranny of the fanatics of Rome. It was Drake who set the country free, took his ships around the world, brought fortunes back to fill the treasury coffers and all the time he was away he would have known that behind his back the Spanish ambassadors would be pouring poison into Elizabeth's ears in an attempt to discredit Drake and his fellow buccaneers. However there came a time when Philip, the Spanish king went too far. He seized an important English ship and flung its crew into dungeons. The Queen was furious. She sent the Earl of Walsingham to see Drake to command him to mark places on a map where Philip was most vulnerable. Drake was wily enough by this time to refuse unless he spoke to the Queen personally. He saw his monarch, she captivated him, and he sailed next time as an admiral with his cabin full of perfumes from the Queen.

The voyage will always rank as the greatest ever achieved. Before Drake returned he had sailed around the world, burst into the secret world of Spain's treasure and acquired knowledge that was to sow the seed of wealth for our merchants beyond their wildest dreams. Drake and his men sailed through terrific storms amid squalls and currents that buffeted their ships and for two months they drifted without sails in waters that no man had mapped before. One of the three ships foundered, another deserted but Drake and his Golden Hind sailed on. After 53 days the storms abated and Drake stood on the deck of his ship watching the waters of the Atlantic rolling into the Pacific. He anchored among islands that had never been recorded. It is said that he landed on the farthest island and walked alone to the end of it. He lay down and threw his arms around the southernmost point of the whole known world.

Drake sailed home triumphant stopping on the way picking up silver, exploring ports, calling at Lima and Panama. They entered Lima alongside a bewildered Spanish ship. In one town they found the Law Courts sitting, kidnapped the judges and took them to the ship. Here they were orderd to clear the town whilst the Golden Hind revictualled. The Spanish were terrified. Philip offered forty thousand pounds to any man who would kidnap or kill El Drake.

Drake was no longer a pirate but the hero of England and the favourite of the Queen. She went to Deptford for the sole purpose of knighting him aboard the Golden Hind. He was rich and powerful but still he made his voyages. He was the only man who could get crews together without the press gang. The beating of the Spanish Armada will probably rank in history as his finest achievement but Drake did so much more for England, and Tavistock should never forget him.

The sense of adventure still lives in the peaceful town. Modernisation takes place at a steady pace but generally gently. Probably the greatest shock to the traders has been the opening of the new Safeway superstore. Situated almost opposite the cemetery on the outskirts of the town, it has done a lot of damage to small shopkeepers. One told me that his shop on the Whitchurch road was down by six hundred pounds a week. I haven't any doubt that supermarkets are invaluable but I hope it will not destroy the essence of Tavistock's life. One of the pleasantest things for any visitor is being able to wander along Duke Street into Brook Street and see a variety of shops offering quality goods. Here there is a wealth of skills and a system that makes the community united.

As you drive in from the direction of Plymouth there is the fine statue of Francis Drake showing him with his treasured mariner's compass in his hand. He stands on a massive granite pedestal which depict scenes from his life. There is Queen Elizabeth knighting him on the Golden Hind; the famous game of bowls on Plymouth Hoe; and his last voyage into the unknown during which he died and was buried at sea. He gazes down the road to the medieval Parish church of St Eustachius which dominates the centre of Tavistock. It has a fine pinnacled tower, a wide nave and many gables. A place of beauty and serenity, much used and much loved. The three gracious aisles lie within lofty arches on slender columns. One of the aisles built for the Clothworkers Guild has a wonderful roof of carved beams and bosses and innumerable angels on the wall plates. St Eustachius was not a lucky man; a Roman officer, he suffered almost as many misfortunes as Job but this church must be his reward. The font is 550 years old but the records of the church do not go back as far, and so we cannot prove whether or not Drake was baptised here. The vicar is John Rawlings, a man who for some years was a Naval Padre and his wealth of experience now brought to this Parish, is welcomed and used to the greatest advantage.

The Parish church has a great deal to do with the life of Tavistock. Apart from its many activities within the church it is also very active in the life of the Church Schools, St Rumon's Infants School in Dolvin Road and St Peter's Junior School at Greenlands. The children come to services in the church and a very real effort is applied to stir their interest in religion in ways that make God and Jesus Christ very much more real than they ever were to me as a child.

Not only the Church Schools use the church, it is used by the two Public Schools, Kelly College and Mount House, which are so much a part of the life of Tavistock. However it was the Abbey that dominated Tavistock way before the Parish church. To all intents and purposes it governed the town and its markets so when Henry VIII gave the Abbey estates to his friend, John Russell, the first Earl of Bedford, it must have meant considerable change. By this time the trade in wool had brought the town new life and prosperity, and everything went swimmingly until the Civil War when the town was held for Parliament by the Earl of Bedford but changed hands no less than six times.

You can still see the stones of the old abbey in the heart of the town square laid out by the Duke of Bedford, who spent his mining royalties in doing so. In the garden of the vicarage across the road from the church the most picturesque fragments of the abbey remain with the Great Gate and the abbot's prison in the ruined tower above it. Betsy Grimbal's Tower is here. She was a nun who was loved by a monk. He, perhaps from a sense of guilt, perhaps rejection, murdered her. Legend tells us that whenever there is any threat to the security of Tavistock or a disaster is impending, a face will appear at one of the windows in the tower.

So much happened here. One of the young abbots became so great, he was chosen to crown William the Conqueror. One of the first printing presses in the country was set up here, and in the medieval church I have witnessed the sadness of death when a young American girl buried her mother beneath its wonderful pinnacled tower, wide nave and glorious gables, and some years later came back across the Atlantic to marry an American in the same church.

I have a great affinity with THE BEDFORD HOTEL in the cellars of which is still the original floor of the abbey. The hotel stands on the site of the ancient Tavistock Abbey built by the Benedictine monks and its quiet dignity reminds you of the past. Here is a hotel that is a small gem in the bejewelled crown of the Forte empire. It must be one their smallest hotels but certainly one of their most interesting. John Barker is the general manager and not only is he enthusiastic about his hotel, he is equally enthusiastic about his adoptive town, Tavistock.

He generously gave me his time to talk about the hotel. It goes without saying that it is comfortable, well appointed and has a high standard of service and catering. One of the disadvantages is its lack of big public rooms which would allow for the very many functions that Tavistock requires annually. Sadly because of its lack of size such occasions have to be catered for elsewhere away from the town. I can see that is frustrating from a business point of view but for me it is the intimate air of the hotel that makes it particularly appealing. The staff all care, from the receptionists who welcome you whether it is for a drink, a meal or to stay, to the man who looks after the plethora of hanging baskets and the car park at the rear. Its position will not allow it to increase in size - it has already used every available space and in so doing had to lose its rather grand and very ornate ballroom which in the last century will have entertained ladies in their ball gowns and their correctly attired escorts.

The Bedford Inn as it was came into being in the middle of the 18th century and had some interesting landlords. One, William Skinner seemed to fall foul of the local bigwigs in 1757 when his license was rescinded because he was 'selling at low rates great quantities of Gin and other common spirits whereby the poor have not only been frequently intoxicated themselves but in consequence thereof through disorder or idleness have with their families either become chargeable to the Parish, or have been reduced to very great want'.

William Skinner's successor, David Depear, offended even more deeply. A letter from Jonathan Jago on the 18th January 1760 said,

'I fear the poor man hath not been entirely blameless. Tho' tis said he will drink, I never heard he was idle or drunken, but on the contrary remarkably diligent, active and tractable whenever company is in the house. The greatest, nay ye only fault I have ever heard objected to him as an Innkeeper is in the badness of the cookery and their great indelicacy in providing entertainments, which of late hath been so remarkable that I have been informed by ye Gentlemen of ye Militia that tho' they frequently desired him to be a little more careful in that particular, mere necessity obliged them against their will to leave his house as his meat in general was scarcely eatable.'

It was not until 1822 that the building currently known as the Bedford Hotel opened its doors to great acclaim. Here was a building that was to add to the prestige of Tavistock and encourage more travellers. The opening was of sufficient importance to warrant a report in The Times which said 'an excellent Inn has been lately built in the gothic style at Tavistock at the expense of the Duke of Bedford, and it is understood to be in the contemplation of his Grace to restore in the same style, the exterior of the most interesting part of the remains of the Abbey.' The hotel also mounted its own advertising campaign which told the public that apart from the comfort of its bedrooms, the excellence of its cuisine and wines, and the distinction of its public rooms, there were also neat post chaises, able horses, excellent stabling and lock up Coach houses.

Quite incorrectly the architecture was attributed to John Foulston, who in 1830 was to be responsible for the ballroom, but the hotel design was left to the much more eminent architect Jeffry Wyatt who was also responsible for the transformation of Windsor Castle in 1824. Foulston had done a considerable amount of work for the Duke of Bedford in Tavistock which is where the confusion arose.

The hotel continued to attract attention and in 1868 it was described thus: 'The Bedford Hotel occupies part of the site of the old edifice and presents an aspect of antiquity - like a full size castle arising phoenix-like out over the ruins of a cathedral.'

The most unhappy time for the hotel was just post-World War II when it was becoming run down. It was still a meeting place but the food was not good and the bedrooms shabby. Tragedy struck the Bedford family when, in 1953, the twelfth Duke was found dead in the grounds of Endsleigh, near Milton Abbot, as a result of a shooting accident. After 400 years the Bedford estates were enormously valuable and stood at about 8 million pounds. The tax man lay in waiting looking for over half this sum in death duties. This resulted in the inevitable sale of some of his properties including Endsleigh and the Bedford Hotel. In May 1955 the local Council purchased the Bedford and used the gardens to make a car park. Needed for the town, but a sad loss to the hotel. However they did not wish to retain the hotel and put it up for auction. It did not reach its reserve price when it came under the hammer in September. It was then that Forte or Trusthouse Forte as it was then, offered 19,000 for it. The offer was accepted and from that day on the hotel has had a new lease of life. It is loved, and cared for and results in the charm it has for business people who enjoy its peace after a day's business, for those who come to stay to explore Dartmoor and for those of us who just enjoy calling in to meet friends, for a good meal or even just a cup of coffee, a lunchtime Bar snack or a wicked Cream Tea.

Tavistock at one time had 22 hostelries. That number is much diminished but over the years I have enjoyed the hospitality of three in particular. In West Street is THE CORNISH ARMS which has won numerous awards for its fare and for six days a week - not Sundays - three female chefs produce some super dishes including my favourite 'Dartmoor Savoury Hot Pot'. Under the same ownership is the attractive BARNABY'S WINE BAR which specialises in Mexican food.

Across the road from The Cornish Arms is the old coaching house, THE QUEENS HEAD with its big welcoming bars, good food and comfortable, inexpensive accommodation. One of the most recent to open is THE ORDULPH ARMS on Kilworthy Hill. Named after the founder of the Benedictine Abbey, it is approximately 80 yards from the Square and is one of Tavistock's many listed buildings. Once it was a temperance hotel and then council offices but in 1983 in the capable hands of Andrew and Richard Coad, it became this delightful pub. Food is very important at the Ordulph and you can eat either in the restaurant or the bar. The home-made dishes, cooked with fresh local produce, are equally good in either.

At No 23 West Street, Mr McDowall owns and runs KOUNTRY KIT, the Outdoor Shop. Here you can buy everything for the outdoors from Boots to fit every type of foot, breathable Waterproof Jckets, waterproofs, clothing, camping and caravan accessories and tents. The motto of the store is 'Stay warm, dry and comfortable from toddler to XXL.' It is a friendly establishment and genuinely tries to fulfil every need for every size.

Exploring the heart of Tavistock is fascinating. In the shadow of Drake's statue in Plymouth Road is the restored Fitzford Gatehouse, all that is left of the Fitz's Tudor Mansion. There is a macabre story told about it and one I have mentioned in a previous chapter but not connected to this Gatehouse. On certain nights of the year, a coach made of bones and drawn by headless horses comes out from the gate and within is a beautiful female ghost. The coach and horses are led by a vicious dog with only one eye, set in the middle of its forehead. They travel as far as Okehampton churchyard, where the lady descends, plucks a blade of grass, clutches it to herself, boards the coach and orders the coachman to return to Fitzford gate. The lady is supposedly Lady Howard doing penance for murdering her four husbands. If you are of a literal mind and demand facts, the story cannot be completely true - she only murdered three of her four husbands, the fourth escaped! All these ghostly happenings do not seem to perturb the people who live contentedly in Fitzford Cottages alongside the gate.

West Street runs behind the church and has on its corner just across from St Eustachius, the fine imposing building of Hurdwick stone which houses LLOYDS BANK. Hurdwick stone which has a strange green tinge to it is much used in Tavistock and lends a gracious air to the buildings. Also in West Street is the very useful and efficient GB PROPERTY MANAGEMENT who look after property for people and also organise lettings. A surprising number of people in the Tavistock area make use of this service as well as those who have moved away and know that they can leave their houses in GB's capable hands.

The main street nearest to the Square is Duke Street which then runs immediately into Brook Street. Behind Duke Street is the busy Pannier Market which seems to have stalls everywhere. Every Tuesday the market is devoted to Antiques, Collectables, Bric-a-Brac and high quality Hand Crafted Wares. Wednesday is the day for the Victorian Fair - an interesting and varied range of wears and wares presented by traders in period dress. Every Friday is the traditional Charter Market providing food, general needs and requirements. Saturday is like an Aladdin's Cave with a 'Nothing New' day on the first Saturday in the month. The last Saturday is the same as a Victorian Wednesday Market.

The indoor market hall is crammed and frequently the stalls spill over into the street outside. It is all go and bustle and has an atmosphere of well being that is totally divorced from the miseries of recession. Everyone, traders and customers, chatter away and then disappear for a well earned cup of tea or coffee either at one of the tables laid out on the perimeter road or just along Duke and Brook Street which both have several establishments. One Coffee House in Brook Street I enjoy especially in the summer when one can sit out in the little garden.

Fruit and vegetables always look so much fresher and tempting in the market and in the busy vegetable shop just at the beginning of Duke Street. I have always been able to buy the unusual there, even in the days before supermarkets existed and Aubergine was an unknown! Artists and craftspeople bring their work to the market for sale. It is not hard to find some beautiful designer knitwear or a cuddly toy. Home-made cakes are always a temptation to me and so are secondhand bookstalls. In fact the market is somewhere in which I am happy to browse.

Another place which exerts a powerful attraction for me is THE TAVISTOCK AUCTION ROOMS in Market Road. Once a fortnight there is a sale of household goods. You can rummage around the day before, probably just as well because all sorts of things turn up, and on the day of the sale the room is so full it is almost impossible to see the lots as they are called. The auctioneer works briskly, seems to know a good many of the regulars by their first names and has an unerring eye for a likely bidder, so don't scratch your nose by mistake!

Market Street has most of the period houses of the town and it is said that King Charles used the old Chevalier House as his headquarters at some time during the Civil War.

Bedford Square is graced by the Town Hall with its battlements and pinnacles. Completed in 1860 it has a beautiful vaulted ceiling and can seat 500 people. The main function rooms all reflect the life of Tavistock, and there are some fine portraits of the Bedford family, Lord John Russell and Sir Francis Drake. This is an ideal venue for dinner dances, wedding receptions, parties, exhibitions, sales, mini-conferences and theatrical productions. It has been equipped with modern kitchens in recent years and is capable of producing a multi-course meal for 200 guests. That it is a popular venue goes without saying.

The Guildhall was rebuilt in 1848 and with its pinnacles and battlements was obviously the inspiration for the Town Hall. It is used now for Magistrate Sittings and in front of it stands the local granite memorial which honours the men and women of the town who gave their lives in World War I and World War II.

The present Town Council offices in Drake Road, where I met the well respected Town Clerk, Don Bent, also house a small, fascinating museum which portrays the life of the town and especially the town's Industrial Revolution.

Duke Street has the well established PILLARS, a newsagents which has been there as long as I can remember. It sells not only papers but all manner of things and is a fountain of information for any visitor wanting to know something about the town and its people. It has stood on the same site since 1860 and was originally a printers specialising in memorial printing for deceased miners. I can remember a time when it had a link with The Lidstone Advertising Company in Plymouth who used to do the majority of billposting in the South West. If my memory is correct Pillars used to print some of the posters. No doubt one of the two families who have owned this thriving business during the last 134 years will remember. One should never think about Pillars being antique - quite the reverse - they have moved with the times and the business now embraces new technology. The enthusiasm for the business as well as its professionalism has brought them national recognition as the National Newsagent of the Year for 1990.

At number 14 is DARTMOOR PHOTOGRAPHIC with an excellent range of cameras, films, albums, an instant Passport Service and for holiday makers, a one hour film processing. In the same building is the long established SEW 'N' SO owned and run by Barbara Porter whose motto is 'If it can be sewn, we can do it.' Over the years she has built up a large clientele who know that she can be relied on to do immaculate tailoring alterations, sew in a recalcitrant zip, design and make well cut dresses and other garments as well as creating some interesting curtains and drapes. Her husband who works with her has a fascinating machine which turns out personalised machine embroidery.

The need for good taxation and accounting services is met by MICHAEL TAYLOR TAXATION AND ACCOUNTING SERVICES at Number One Duke Street. Michael Taylor offers an efficient friendly service to his clients whether it is help in preparing VAT and PAYE, personal or business taxation. Small businesses particularly find the company invaluable.

Dress shops with differing styles are many, some run of the mill and one or two with clothes to delight anyone who can afford a few pounds more than most. Essentially 'county' in their merchandise they attract people from far and wide. Menswear on the other hand is in short supply so it is particlularly fortunate that at Number 12 Brook Street FARLEY'S MENSWEAR offers so much. This is a truly traditional establishment catering for males of every age group. The beautifully presented window, which I first spotted sitting across the road in one of the several very good coffee shops, is the work of the three female owners, Valerie, Anne and Sue. The doors were first opened twenty five years ago and these skilled, courteous and enthusiastic ladies have been in situ since just before the Christmas of 1976. They have seen fashion change tremendously, and have always kept up with the current trends, but never to the detriment of traditional standards.

Farley's clientele comes from all over the country as well as local people. It is a regular shopping place for visitors who come to Tavistock and know that they will find many of their favourite brands of shirts, sweaters, trousers, sports jackets, casual wear and accessories. If you cannot find your size in any particular style, you will find the ladies very willing to try and obtain whatever is required.

Tradition is something also associated with CREBERS, the Harrod's Food Hall of Tavistock. This splendid shop was established in 1881 and has been with the same family ever since. It has a modern staff with old fashioned standards, it stocks anything from Cornflakes to Caviar, an old Claret or an inexpensive wine. It has a cheese counter which will delight the taste buds and encourage you to be adventurous. It is somewhere that is a delight to shop.

For many years Creber's have been sending hampers and gift parcels all over this country and abroad, especially at Christmas. Each hamper is packed to the customer's requirements and recently they have introduced a gift voucher service.

I spent a very constructive and happy hour or so with the editor of the TAVISTOCK TIMES GAZETTE, a newspaper that reports local events and takes a keen interest in all that goes on in Tavistock. Colin Brent is the editor who is also responsible for a similar paper in Okehampton. This well informed man works with a small, competent team in almost Dickensian offices but with equipment that is as up to date as the biggest newspaper. The policy of the paper is one of constructive service to the community and follows very much the brief set out by the owner of the Tindle Group to whom the paper belongs. That the method is successful and worthwhile is proven by the fact that the owner Ray Tindle, received a knighthood in the Queen's Birthday Honours list.

I sat awhile waiting to see Colin on a day when this weekly paper was being put 'to bed'. His working space is at the back of a small shop in Brook Street, which serves as a meeting place for locals who kept on coming in to place their advertisments and have a chat at the sametime with the cheerful lady behind the counter. As a first class means of communication within the community The Tavistock Times is an excellent example.

There is a pretty mews off Brook Street in Paddons Row. Here I discovered SECRETS which is a browser's paradise and specialises in Bonsai. It is this sort of discovery that makes Tavistock so interesting. At 10, Brook Street in THE VILLAGE SHOPPING ARCADE there is another shopping experience. Here you will find COUNTRY CLOTHES with a wide range of jumpers, trousers, skirts and wet weather wear. THE MONSTER SANDWICH CO offers freshly cut sandwiches, as well as some delicious and distinctly fattening West Country Fudge. There are chocolates, luscious ice cream and a range of gifts. MOTHER GOOSE is devoted to the raising of money for Plymouth's St Luke's Hospice. It is a Charity Shop and does very well. BOZ offers secondhand books. TAVISTOCK JEWELLERY BOX has a fascinating selection of Gold, Silver and individual Fashion Jewellery.

THE TAVISTOCK SADDLERY will appeal to anyone looking for something for the horse and rider and also has a first class repair service for Leatherwork. It took me back years when I walked into LOOSEWEIGH FOOD SHOP. Here rice and spices, dried fruits and mixes are not done up in uninteresting packets but weighed out and sold in the old fashioned manner - I am old enough to remember the days when a Grocers shop had a counter, and on the customer side there were chairs where one could sit whilst being served or placing an order which would be delivered by an errand boy on his bike. I'm not sure how HABI-DABI-CRAFTS acquired its name but it sounds like magician's magic. Inside it lives up to that image with anything from Tapestry for a Baronial Hall to a beloved Teddy needing an eye. BARE NECESSITIES offers natural beauty products produced without cruelty to animals, and last but not least, is THE WOOL SHOP with every kind of wool for keen knitters as well as some very pretty hand knitted baby clothes.

I could go on for quite a long time about the benefits and pleasures of shopping in this delightful old town but there is much more. The council have moved with the times as is witnessed in the excellent MEADOWLANDS LEISURE POOL on The Wharf. Here you are dared to Ride the River Rapids, go through the Wild Water, Zoom the Tube, or relax in the Spa Pool where you can listen to the Waterfalls and Fontains cascading into the pool. Children love their own Pool with its Bubble Seat, Water Cannons, Rain Shower. Frequently Birthday Parties are held here. It is enjoyable to eat in the Beachcomber which overlooks the pool.

Tavistock offers many services. It goes without saying that the town has all the normal collection of builders, decorators, plumbers etc, all with expertise and a pride both in their work and the town. It also has much to do with agriculture. ABBEY GARDEN MACHINERY on The Crelake Industrial Estate, Pixon Lane, for example. Here you can purchase Garden machinery, bring it in for servicing and repair or, if needs be, hire. All makes of Farm and estate Machinery are also serviced and repaired and parts manufactured as required for older machines. Mr John and his team are sensible, competent people and fully aware of the need to run an efficient service.

Caring for Nursery school age children is the responsibility of the cheerful, loving and happy SUNNINGDALE NURSERY at 54 Plymouth Road. The Nursery which has just celebrated its tenth anniversary is housed in a beautiful Victorian building opposite the Meadows. There are six warm, bright welcoming playrooms, using cheerful colours and simple layout which give ample opportunity for imaginative and constructive play. There is a well stocked library of over 400 books, table toys, puzzles and construction sets to encourage hand and eye co-ordination. Water, clay, painting, drawing, music, cooking, woodwork and gardening all help develop skills and concepts for the basis of later learning. Hot wholefood lunches are provided for children who want to stay and then in the afternoons there is a less formal routine which might well include a visit to the Meadows to feed the ducks.

I was impressed with the use of the gardens in which there are two grassed areas and numerous flower beds, a wooden playhouse, two sand pits and a large playground with a simple road layout to teach the basics of Road Safety, and makes the riding of the many tricycles, scooters and pedal cars more interesting.

The Nursery fills the void between playgroup and Primary School, with its offer of nursery education to the three to five year olds. There is a high ratio of qualified and experienced staff who with their knowledge, enthusiasm and love of children, encourages and extends the potential of each individual child within this caring environment. They see the Nursery as the child's workplace and in many ways a home from home,

where the tranquil atmosphere induces the childs natural love of learning. Many of these children will go on to be locally educated in Tavistock's highly respected schools. The church schools I have mentioned already but there is also TAVISTOCK COLLEGE, a super Comprehensive School, with a go ahead headmaster who is bringing acclaim to the educational standards. TAVISTOCK PRIMARY SCHOOL in Plymouth Road and WHITCHURCH JUNIOR SCHOOL create in their pupils the desire to learn and to be successful wherever they continue their education.

Unusually for such a small town, Tavistock has two Public Schools, MOUNT HOUSE SCHOOL in Mount Tavy Road which is a Boys Preparatory School of great repute, housed in a wonderful setting. Here boys are encouraged to develop their talents, learn to be self reliant and at the same time to have the natural exuberance of youth channelled into useful pursuits.

The dignified KELLY COLLEGE, set in beautiful grounds and amidst playing fields stands across the valley from Mount House. Christopher Hirst, the comparatively young headmaster, runs this school with an iron hand in a velvet glove. He and his experienced, dedicated staff have an excellent relationship with the pupils under their care. Probably a totally different approach from Admiral Benedictus Kelly who founded the school in 1877 as a public school for 'sons of Naval Officers and other gentlemen'. The lessening of the Armed Forces has meant a lessening of the number of serving officers' sons but the ties with the Services is still very strong. Today's pupils, many of whom come to school daily, and do not board, are a different breed. In the last few years the school has become co-educational successfully. Christopher Hirst told me that the first year was the most difficult when the boys had mixed feelings about sharing their school with females and the girls were unsure of themselves. Now it has produced a sort of civilising effect on both sexes.

What is deemed to be most important at Kelly is the small classes enabling the teachers to give individual attention and also cultivates self discipline. The academic results speak for themselves.

Kelly College offers much more than just academia. Its sports facilities are superb and its record against other schools in every aspect is outstanding. They expect to win medals! Probably the school's swimming pool is better known than anything else. It was here that Gold Medalist, Sharon Davis, did so much of her training. The pool is also used as a swimming club by the people of Tavistock.

Some may wonder at, and dislike the idea of their offspring being sent away to school, but for most children it gives them a chance to spread their wings and become strong individuals. I have just seen this metamorphosis happen with my nine year old grandson, who had a dreadful time at his day school where the classes were large, and little was done to stimulate his mind and help his limited concentration. He hated the school and they despaired of him. His first year at a preparatory school as a boarder has seen him blossom. This underlines the great benefit of smaller classes, one of the specialities of Kelly College.

Choosing the right school for your child is so important. There was a time when it was as sure as night will follow day that sons would follow their fathers into the same school. Now, whilst that is great for tradition, it is not always the best for the child. I was impressed by Christopher Hirst's ability to move with the times and to make sure that every pupil in his care was encouraged to develop their own especial talents and likings. Music, for example; a subject sometimes pushed to one side by a school with a great sporting tradition. Here it flourishes and achieves as much for thosewho play as it does for those who show their prowess on the field of sport.

Kelly's interest in the affairs of Tavistock is much appreciated locally. Not only does its very presence aid the economy of the town, it also provides assistance with many projects. I was delighted to hear that the school were about to help the struggling AMBULANCE MUSEUM, once housed in Plymouth and now at the old Tate and Lyle site just outside Tavistock on the Okehampton Road.. This is a very worthwhile scheme. Not only will it help to get the Ambulance Museum better known, it also aims to assist in the making of Nature Trails on the site. For those who know nothing about the Ambulance Museum, do go and take a look. There is an amazing display of every type of Ambulance from the days when a litter was the only means of carrying wounded soldiers. Each of the vehicles has been lovingly restored by Trevor Hall with his team of voluntary helpers, and brought to such a state that they are all show pieces and in frequent demand for films, documentaries.

Writing letters to every Television and Theatre Production Company was time consuming but it brought Trevor results. The ambulances have found their way into the House of Elliot and Doctor Finlay, a 1951 Bedford ML2 was used in one of the Miss Marple series, and the producers of Indiana Jones used a 1938 Opal Blitz ambulance which served in the Spanish Civil War.

'We are such stuff as dreams are made of' always comes to mind when I think about Trevor Hall and his Ambulance Museum. Just a few years ago he was a member of the Ambulance Service, a man with a desire to get children to have a better understanding of what the service did. He found and bought an old ambulance and started taking it to schools, in his own time and at his own expense. Once there he caught their attention and imagination. It was not long before a teacher told him she knew where he could get another ambulance. Someone else told him where he could lay his hands on equipment to fit out the inside. The germ of the dream was sown. Before long the possession of a number of ambulances dating as far back as 1830 took too much of his spare time, and so he made the brave decision to resign from the Ambulance Service and start activating his dream - a full scale ambulance museum. Each step of the way has been fraught because of the lack of money but Trevor Hall has persevered and those who see the result of his efforts, find the experience fascinating. The one thing that stops this innovative museum, the only one in Europe, if not the world, from becoming a highflyer is the lack of any kind of sponsor or grant. Everything is done on a shoe string and so the help on offer from Kelly is a Godsend.

KELLY COLLEGE

Kelly College does not let traditions disappear. Attendance in the school's own chapel is compulsory as is a period spent in the combined Cadet Force; something which is enjoyed by almost everyone.

There is a gentle feeling throughout Kelly College. Something not quite tangible but from the moment you enter the main gate off the Tavistock-Okehampton Road, pass the Lodge and drive slowly onwards to the car park at the top of a hill, you are aware of this sense of wellbeing. The grounds are superb, the buildings sometimes dignified, sometimes newish and growing into the scene. It is a school to be proud of and I cannot imagine any pupil ever being unhappy here.

Tavistock has so much going on all the time but I suppose it is things agricultural which are predominant. The busy Livestock Cattle Market on the Whitchurch Road is a good insight into farming life. Here on market days you will find it buzzing. The open space at the wide junction of Down Road becomes a busy car park. There are members of the farming fraternity everywhere, frequently speaking a language that is almost foreign to the layman. The noise is incredible. I can never understand how the auctioneer can hear bids. I am told that it is more than your life is worth to sit in a farmer's usual place. You may think the seat is empty but watch out for a walking stick suspended on the circular railing just in front of the seat. That is the 'engaged' sign.

In addition to the weekly markets there are also several Fairs every year. The most famous is Goosey Fair. It comes on the second Wednesday in October, at a time when Tavistock is settling down for the winter and saying farewell to visitors from all over the world. Then it is the turn of those of us from Plymouth and all over Devon and Cornwall to descend on the town for this unique occasion. It is supposed to be just a one day fair and from a point of view of the selling of wares that is so, but the excitement builds as the stallholders keep on arriving during the previous day, claiming their pitches in the Square and all along Pymouth Road. Each one has been given a pitch number which is marked out in large white numbers on the pavement. It is a time for the meeting of old friends, time for a drink or two before the evening arrives and the stalls need erecting. There are always huge numbers of people milling around watching all the activity and anticipating the fun of the fair.

The following morning, very early, Goosie Fair is open and people pour into the town. Children have no school on this day and you see their wide eyed appreciation of the stalls, the fair, the candyfloss and everything that goes with this sort of happening. The pubs are open all day and do a roaring trade. Goose is on the menu everywhere from a traditional Goose dinner to a Goose sarnie. You can buy just about anything from china to goldfish. It is a day of fun, laughter, music and noise. Everyone is determined to enjoy it come rain or shine - frequently it is the former for Tavistock is reputed to be one of the wettest places in the county! Goosie Fair is essentially Tavistocks. It has been an annual event for as long as anyone can remember. Certainly a never to be forgotten experience.

Returning to a little more sanity, I suggest a visit to THE TAVISTOCK TROUT FARM at Mount Tavy, known locally as Abbi's place after the owner, Abigail Underhill, whose father dug the ponds himself 15 years ago. Its a fascinating place where one can just go and look or purchase if you will. When you hear the conversation of other people around you, you realise that Abbi has a clientele from much further afield than Tavistock. She told me that she has regular customers locally, fishermen from all over the country and a vast number of visitors who come to Tavistock during the season. It is a welcoming place and somewhere from which one can learn a lot about trout. Abigail encourages the questions and interest of youngsters and will patiently answer everything she is asked.

One would not class visiting or catching trout on a Trout Farm a really sporting activity but Tavistock has much to offer in this field. The rivers around Tavistock are well stocked and permits can be obtained for both salmon and trout fishing. Anglers can obtain licences from the River Authority. On Whitchurch Down, Tavistock Golf Club has a superb 18 hole course with wonderful views of Dartmoor. Out on the Brentor Road is another, the Hurdwick Golf Club. Cricket is another favourite pastime and the town has a first class pitch at the Ring on Whitchurch Down.

There are riding stables, badminton, archery, tennis, bowls, hockey, football, rugby, squash and rifle clubs. Each has its devotees and you have only to read the Tavistock Times Gazette to see what a competitive lot the people of Tavistock are.

Tavistock is a friendly, relaxed community, delighted to entertain visitors and to share the beauty of their town.

BETSY GRIMBAL'S TOWER

ABBEY RUINS

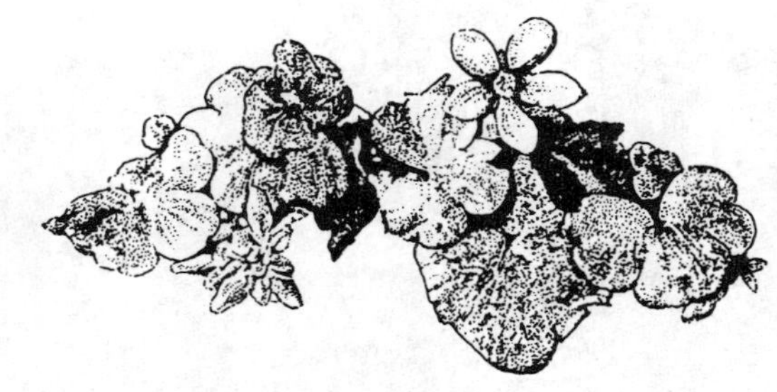

There was a time, not so long ago, when traffic made Okehampton a nightmare but new roads and bypasses have allowed it to return to the pleasant somnolence of a country market town selling the agricultural produce of the surrounding area. I often feel that Okehampton, rightly named the northern Gateway to Dartmoor, does not get the attention it deserves from visitors who do not recognise that it is a superb centre for touring and exploring Dartmoor, and an interesting place in its own right. The moors rise behind the town, sometimes friendly and sometimes menacing but always beckoning those who like to walk and discover its magic.

This is where the two Okement rivers meet, where the Cornish born poet, Sydney Godolphin is buried in the church. Born in 1610 he went to Oxford at 14 and to Parliament at 18. Had he not been so active in so many fields he would undoubtedly have written more verse but he has left us with poetry of distinction. He was a romantic, a Christian and a Royalist. With the outbreak of the Civil War he retired to Cornwall and raised a body of men to stand for the King. He was shot dead in a skirmish at Chagford when he was only 32. My imaginative mind working overtime often wonders when I am reading or writing about him, if he was one of the Cavaliers who fought the Roundheads on Fingle Bridge.

Okehampton lays claim to a famous engineer born here in 1799. James Meadows Rendel was a farmer's son, who from an early age wanted to be a builder of bridges. He went to London and learnt to survey under the tutelage of the great Telford, for whom he worked on the plans of a suspension bridge across the Mersey. It was Rendel who designed Brixham Harbour and the Breakwater at Torquay. Canals fascinated him and he was responsible for the plans of many.

The parish church of Okehampton stands on a hill and is of the 19th century. The original was destroyed in a disastrous fire which left only the tower and its six bells. Tree lined avenues lead up to the church and one is almost paved with 17th century gravestones amongst which is one of a French prisoner of war. There is a monument to Benjamin Gayer with the vestry. A Mayor of Okehampton, who in 1701 was convicted of sheep stealing and hanged He is reputed to haunt Cranmere Pool, and if there ever was a Pool at Cranmere, then the blame for its disappearance must lie with him. His spirit was banished to Cranmere Pool, to remain there until he had drained it - using a sieve! His phantom, in the form of a black pony, is still known to make occasional appearances. St Andrews is a well cared for church and stands away from the traffic unlike the little 15th century chapel of St James in the centre of the town which must shake in its ancient foundations as lorries rumble by.

Probably one of the best ways to explore Okehampton is to pick up a copy of THE TOWN TRAIL from the Information Centre. You will find on your voyage of discovery that Dartmoor, with land available for stock farming was the reason why people first came here. Prehistoric and Iron Age peoples settled in this area. Later on, the Romans, acknowledging Okehampton's strategic position on the route from the South east to the South west, built a road to link Exeter and Cornwall and a small fort to guard the river crossing. The Celts, who named the river the Okement, which means swift and noisy, lived here too. While the Saxons, in their hilltop settlement on the site of the present parish church, lived in a place called Ocmundtune.

The castle built by the Normans gave the area its major importance within the west country. Their castle was given a commanding position overlooking the town and the surrounding countryside. Gradually Ocmundtune was abandoned in favour of the new town which developed in the valley below the castle.

Many of the town's buildings are examples of Victorian and Edwardian architecture: the arcade, almshouses and the Market Hall. The coming of the railway in 1871 encouraged a building boom with many new houses being constructured, while much of the old town was restored to the fine three storey buildings you can see today. Over the centuries charters were granted allowing the election of officials, special courts, markets and fairs. The town was allowed two M.P's and these included famous names like William Pitt the elder and Clive of India.

The trail starts in the courtyard of THE MUSEUM OF DARTMOOR LIFE leaving which you turn left along West Street crossing West Bridge which was an original fording place of the Okement river. The old road to Cornwall ran up the high Street. From the bridge you can see various old inns which underline Okehampton's position as a staging post on the high road from London to Cornwall, and the 'New Road' which was cut in the 19th century. If you have time by crossing the road and turning right up Church Street and then along the cobbled Choir Boys Path you arrive at the Parish Church. From here you have lovely views of the town and the surrounding countryside. Walking back along Ranelagh Road you join Lodge Hill. At this junction is Okehampton's only surviving toll house, 'Bus House'.

The octagonal building at the bottom of Lodge Hill was the gothic lodge to Oatlands House and crossing the bridge you enter Market Street, formerly the site of the livestock market. The present Market Hall is still used for numerous events,including a Saturday 'pannier' market. The Charter Hall next door was built in 1973 to commemorate the renewal of the town's charter of 1623. The Town Hall on the corner of Fore Street is made of granite and was built as a town house for a local merchant and M.P. It became the Town Hall in 1821 and still retains the original oak staircase. There is also a very fine council Chamber. Next door is the Red Lion Yard shopping precinct which was designed to blend in with older buildings on the site. At number 7 look for a display of Teddy Bears in a Dolls House Minature setting.

Fore Street is the main shopping street of Okehampton. Crossing the road from the Town Hall you can investigate the various shops inside the Arcade, and at the top end by turning left along St James Street you come to St James Chapel probably the town's best known landmark. In the past the chapel was used by townspeople unable to reach the Parish Church in times of flood and its best feature is the 14th century tower. The chapel is in the care of trustees on behalf of the town and because of this fact it is described by church authorities as a 'peculiar'. To local people the clock and its chimes are a feature of daily life. The custom of ringing evening curfew from the tower only lapsed about 30 years ago: a link with feudal times when the ringing of a bell was the signal to put out all fires and lights.

Continue towards East Street and after crossing East Bridge you pass the Fountain Inn, a former coaching inn which has kept its archway through to the stable yard. Then turn right into Mill Road to pass the Town Mill, an early 19th century water mill on a medieval site. The mill is now converted into flats although the waterwheel has been retained.

Walking on down the hill you pass Simmons Park on your left. The park is a lovely place for a stroll and amongst other features it contains a semi-detached lodge in the style of a swiss chalet. It is also the suitable setting for the town's enclosed and heated swimming pool. Sydney Simmons, after whom the Park is named, was born in Okehampton in 1840 and made a fortune in London. Described as ' the man who has the head to make money and the heart to give it away' he gifted the park, the golf links and the castle to the town.

Leaving the park and continuing down the road you can visit Okehampton Castle by following Castle Road on the left. This takes you past Brock's Almshouses and at Castle Hospital which was originally the workhouse, you can either follow the signed footpath to Lover's Meet and cross the footbridge into the Castle Car Park or take the road past the rows of Castle Cottages. Okehampton Castle is both one of the oldest and largest castle's in Devon and has its own visiting ghost. Otherwise to return to the town centre you continue past the Post Office and the Police Station.

The Georgian WHITE HART HOTEL stands solidly opposite the handsome town hall of 1685. The White Hart is named an hotel and certainly has comfortable bedrooms but it is far more a meeting place for local people in the bars, and the function rooms are in great demand for all sorts of local occasions. The food is good traditional fare, the wine list not spectacular but acceptable, and the beer well kept. The hotel is reputed to be haunted by a young boy named Peter who wanders the corridors looking for his murdered mother.

I attended a Farmers Union dinner in the White Hart once with my husband who was the guest of honour. unfortunately because of road works we arrived late and had little chance, before we sat down at table to meet people. I found myself sitting next to a rosy-cheeked mature man, who smiled readily, said little in response to my chatter about farming, apart from the occasional yes or no. I found it hard going but he seemed contented enough. After dinner and the usual speeches I met several other people and eventually asked who my dinner companion was. 'Ah, Joe, good man, stone deaf mind you but one of the shrewdest antique dealers in the county.' All the seeds of my conversation had fallen on stony ground. If he heard anything at all of my conversation, he must have thought I was mad!

Next door to the White Hart, surrounding a pretty cobbled courtyard is THE MUSEUM OF DARTMOOR LIFE which is part of the North Dartmoor Museums Association. Alan Endacott is the Curator and the driving force behind the enterprise. Alan has been in love with Dartmoor from an early age, and a collector of anything remotely connected with the Moor. It is this collection, together with donations from all sorts of people, which has helped to furnish the museum. This particular part of it is set in an old mill and tells the story of the people who have lived and worked on Dartmoor from prehistoric times. Nothing stuffy in the presentation. It is lively and everything is simply explained. In one part there is a reconstruction of domestic and working life, another has displays of minerals and prehistoric relics. Farm implements and vintage vehicles stand by the blacksmith's and wheelwright's shops and there is a fine working waterwheel.

MUSEUM OF DARTMOOR LIFE

Alan and his committee are well aware of the need to keep changing the exhibitions, which makes it the sort of place to which you can come back and find something new everytime. Schools use the centre regularly and one of the museum's main tasks is to ensure that the displays tie in with the national curriculum. September and October 1994 will see a special exhibition launched in celebration of the 500th anniversary of the Stannary Towns with much on tin mining - the reason for the setting up of the Stannary Court.

In addition to the museum there are craft shops in the courtyard. THE OPAL STUDIO has opal and gem cutting demonstrations, plus a wide range of exclusive and inexpensive jewellery, rocks, minerals and leather goods. Guaranteed jewellery repairs are a part of the service as well. One of the memorable moments when you come to the Museum of Dartmoor Life is a visit to the Victorian Tea Rooms where, in addition to the good, old-fasioned Devon home cooking, you are offered one of the best Pavlovas to be had anywhere.

Within the courtyard is THE DARTMOOR VISITORS CENTRE which opens its doors to offer advice and information on where to go and what to do in the area. The people who run it, like Alan Endacott and his colleagues, are all enthusiasts and you will find them very helpful.

You will find in Chapter Two information about an excellent walk that one can take between Okehampton and Sticklepath, part of the Tarka Trail, taking you to the FINCH FOUNDRY MUSEUM at Sticklepath, which comes under the jurisdiction of the National Trust. It is housed in FINCH FOUNDRY, a 19th century waterpowered factory which produced sickles, scythes and shovels. It is quite unique and exhilirating to watch working waterwheels driving the ancient machinery. Recently a Chagford man, Jim Coyne has been appointed custodian. He is an enthusiast and a great motivator who is ably supported by his team of volunteers in the caring for the foundry and museum.

OKEHAMPTON CASTLE is a glorious ruin. Established by the Normans as the seat of the first Sheriff of Devon,the castle was largely rebuilt in the 14th century as a lavish home for the Courtenays, Earls of Devon. No one has lived here since Henry VIII had the castle dismantled, but you can still see the whole plan of the ancient fortificiation, the 15th century entrance tower, banqueting hall, the kitchens, 13th century chapel and the Norman keep. It is in a wonderful woodland setting and you can walk through the old Deer park. I think it is a magical place in which to picnic alongside the river, especially if you have taken advantage of the Soundalive personal stereo tours which fire the imagination and keep you wrapt in the cocoon of history long after the tour is over.

The castle is open from Good Friday - 30th September from 10am-6pm daily and from October until the end of March from 10am-4pm, Tuesday to Sunday.

The town has a weekly newspaper, THE OKEHAMPTON TIMES which is similar in style and format to the successful Tavistock Times Gazette. In fact it has one and the same editor, Colin Brent. It is a good, gossipy paper relating to the happenings both in Okehampton and for several miles around. Buy a copy and you will discover all the local activities, the summer fetes, the car boot sales and a variety of hostelries who will be delighted to welcome you.

In March 1994 the paper opened new offices in St James Street, an occasion graced by the Mayor Sylvia Westlake and the paper's proprietor Ray Tindle who reminded us that his first visit to Okehampton, totally unconnected with newspapers, had been 50 years ago shortly before he enlisted in the Devonshire regiment - the same regiment in which Mrs Westlake's husband, saw wartime service.

The newspaper's office like that of the Tavistock Times Gazette is always a busy place and one in which one gleans quite a lot of what is happening in the Okehampton district. The paper has a lot of local advertisers and you could well see an advertisment for OKEHAMPTON GOVERNMENT SURPLUS WAREHOUSE which offers a huge selection of anything from tents to Chefs Knives and Blankets. There might well be another for THE NATIONAL TRUST telling you of all their properties in Devon which are open for your enjoyment. For opening times and events, it is suggested that you ring the place in question. ARLINGTON COURT, Barnstaple 850296, BUCKLAND ABBEY, Yelverton 853607, CASTLE DROGO, Chagford 433306, KILLERTON HOUSE & GARDEN, Exeter 881345, LYDFORD GORGE, Lydford 441 0r 320, COLETON FISHACRE GARDEN, Kingswear 752466, COMPTON CASTLE, Kingskerswell 872112, KNIGHTSHAYES COURT & GARDEN, Tiverton 254665, OVERBECKS MUSEUM & GARDEN, Salcombe 842893 0r 843238, SALTRAM HOUSE, Plymouth 336546, A LA RONDE, Exmouth 265514. FINCH FOUNDRY, 0837 840046. Each one of these interesting and delightful places is within reasonable reach of Okehampton and certainly worthwhile seeking out. The Okehampton Times advertises and writes about everything. They have a young, go-getter reporter with a keen sense of news and a liking for people and occasions and of course the whole is presided over by the editor, Colin Brent.

There is one lady in Okehampton I would like you to meet. Her name is Jane Seigal who owns HEATHFIELD HOUSE, situated 800 feet above sea level on the outskirts of the town. She runs this country house primarily for people who enjoy the moors. Since she was 18 it has always been her ambition to live on or close to Dartmoor. This objective she achieved when she bought Heathfield House which literally backs onto the edge of the northern part of the moor, well placed for wonderful walks if you are so inclined, or drive for miles amongst the most haunting scenery you will ever see.

Jane has converted quite an ordinary house into a comfortable home, every bedroom has an exceptionally high standard and all are en-suite with either bath or de-luxe power showers. She is a superb cook and housekeeper which one would think would take all her time, but not a bit of it, Jane is so well organised that part of staying at Heathfield is walking with her on the moors, to all her favourite places. She will take you to little known spots and point out to you, on the way, the bird life, which is her great love, as well as the flora and fauna. You will see HIGH WILLHAYS and YES TOR, both 2000ft high and waiting to be climbed. You will hear tell of the ancient legends and much of the folk lore of Dartmoor.

There is no need to feel that you will be expected to go on long walks. Jane is not a bossy walker! You can take walks at your own pace and enjoy them. If she is not with you, she will map a route out for you, or perhaps direct you, somewhere other than the moors. There is so much beauty around Okehampton.

This is a non-smoking house, which I think is a blessing, but one needs to be forewarned. Probably part of the great pleasure in staying at Heathfield is that there are only four rooms so it is never crowded and at night everyone tends to sit around after dinner, sipping a glass of wine and chatting over the day's activities. It may well be that you feel too contented to move anyway after the fabulous meal you will have eaten; one of the few rules of the house is that you must try every one of Jane's delectable desserts!

It is as well to tell you how to find Heathfield House. Travelling west through Okehampton, take the left-hand road at traffic lights. Go past the police station on the left and the post office on the right. Take the next major road on the right (Station Road). Go up this road for 500 yards, keep to the left-hand fork at the fountain. Proceed for another 400 yards and you will see an old railway bridge. Go under the bridge, up a fairly steep road with woods on either side. After approximately 150 yards, the road opens up and there is a little unmade road going slightly left and a small road sharply to the right, but if you continue steeply up the hill, through some rustic wooden gates you will see the house in front of you with a car park to the right.

I would always recommend a drive out to MELDON, west of the town. Make sure you follow the signs to the reservoir and not the quarry! The car park and picnic area has splendid views and it is a good base for a walk alongside the Reservoir or further afield on to the open Moor. You can see the great viaduct and Meldon quarries, where British Rail quarry vast quantities of granite for 'chippings' for the railway tracks. The viaduct once carried the railway line from Tavistock; the line eastwards from Okehampton is still used by the quarry, but no longer carries passengers.

For your evening entertainment Okehampton has its own theatre - The Octagon at Okehampton College, next to Simmons park. It is a 200ft studio theatre which offers a wide variety of entertainment, including music, theatre, film and workshops. You can ring 0837 52001 to find out what is on. The town also has the only cinema for miles around and a night spot with live and disco music. For the energetic, two golf courses welcome visitors, where even beginners are received with open arms. In fact for a small town, Okehampton has much to offer in every department.

To miss CHAGFORD would be a crime. Someone wrote of Chagford in the 1930's 'It is the happiest village in England, for people there never stop smiling. And no wonder, for it lies open to the sun, it is on the threshold of the purple Moor, and at its feet run the brown waters of the Teign, the loveliest of Devon's rivers.' On the face of it, it is a sleepy place, which has grown over the centuries, around its village square. It is a place of charming houses, narrow streets and a sense of well being which has been nurtured over the centuries. Long before the Industrial Revolution created a need for people in the smog ridden towns and cities to find a means of escape and so rediscover the countryside, Chagford catered for the needs of the many small and not so small surrounding villages. It was the 'discovery' of Dartmoor round about 150 years ago that brought visitors to the village. James Perrot, a Chagford man, was probably the first real Dartmoor Guide. He took visitors to CRANMERE POOL from Chagford from the middle of the last century. Even then it was no longer a pool, rather more a bog, but the journey helped to foster in his followers the taste, mystery and allure of Dartmoor. It was he who virtually started Letter Boxing by secreting a bottle at Cranmere Pool, in which his Victorian clients could leave their visiting cards, as proof that they had made the expedition to the heart of the Moor.

Chagford is a little way away from the main routes which gives it a sense of isolation from the wearisome world outside and this comparative seclusion has allowed it to build a community which is quite self-contained and virtually self-sufficient. One of the pamphlets I read before going to Chagford this time said ' The town, unlike so many, does not just come alive for the tourists in the season and then fall back to sleep when they have gone. It has a life of its own, unaltered and unhurried by the rest of the world. Its inhabitants are however, happy to share this timeless quality with their guests.'

If you are hesitant about coming here because of the difficulties of car parking in streets that were never designed for the automobile, do not worry. There is a free car park a few hundred yards from the square. Tinners used to come here from miles around, for it is a Stannary Town and it was here that they would have their precious metal weighed and given the King's Stamp before it was sold. The Royal personage had no objection to this for he received a tax from the tinners! Farmers came here too to sell their cattle and sheep and, in particular, their fleeces. It brings to mind how important the woollen industry was. Everything took place in the market square and watched over by the most distinctive of the town's many historic buildings, the old Market House which stood in the middle. That building has long gone but it was replaced by an octagonal structure which is known affectionately locally as the 'Pepper Pot'. When you see it you will understand why!

RING O'BELLS

It will not take you long to wander around the narrow streets but I will take an even bet that you will be drawn into many amongst the variety of shops, tearooms, a gallery and hostelries, the contents of which will surprise you. There is no way that I can write about them all so just to whet your appetite here are a few. For those with a thirst and looking for a good pub lunch THE RING O'BELLS in the square is a friendly, comfortable establishment which has been offering hospitality to travellers and the locals since the early part of the 17th century. It has an odd history. At one time the back of the inn was used as a mortuary and upstairs became a prison for holding miscreants en route to Okehampton Assizes. Its welcoming walls have not allowed some to escape! To this day there are strange happenings, pictures fall off walls and there are definitely 'bumps in the night: You will find The Ring O' Bells good value whether you are in the mood for a five course feast or a light snack. Judith Pool is the cheery, welcoming 'mine host'.

Also in the square is JAMES BOWDEN & SON founded in 1862 and which can only be described as an emporium! It is quite the most unlikely store to find in a small, moorland town and becomes even more unlikely when you start unravelling the story. It calls itself an ironmongers but you can get every imaginable thing. It is one of the oldest buildings in Chagford and when the great-great-grandfather of the present incumbents started the business, it was known as the Vulcan Ironworks and was a smithy as well as agricultural equipment merchants.

Over the years, through marriage, other family names became associated with the business, as today with Peter Smith who showed me around. In 1910 the Agate family had the local Bellhanging works and were to be seen carting massive bells on carts through the countryside to their destination. The last of these huge bells was hung in Alphington church, now part of Exeter, in 1927. Today it is hard to imagine how such heavy things could be carried, let alone hung, without the modern equipment we take for granted.

Every branch of this amazing family seems to have been innovative, none more so than the Smiths. Peter Smith's grandfather invented 'Silverlight', which few will have heard of, but it was the forerunner of Calor Gas. The work of the smithy went on until 1958. The local hand operated fire engine was also kept on the premises. It was a slightly Harry Tate operation to say the least. If the alarm was raised the horses had to be caught before they were harnessed to the engine. This gave the voluntary firemen time for a quick drink in the nearest hostelry - probably the Ring O' Bells. This was not the most efficient of ideas because by the time they arrived at the scene of the fire, the chances were there was nothing left but charred ruins.

All this information came pouring up out of Peter Smith's memory whilst we sat in a tiny shop museum that he created at the top of the store. All around me were examples of past shopware, from tills to scales, bottles to buttons. Years of local newspapers were stacked in one corner. Much of the material has been given to him by local people. The museum is not always open but if Peter Smith is around he will open the doors and take you in. If not you have to content yourself looking through the glass windows and door that shield all this wonderful memorabilia.

FOWLERS is also in the square. Once known as Rickeards, it is now owned and run by Philip Fowler. This is an Estate Agency operated on the most ethical and helpful lines. Many of his clients come from quite a distance away and in seeking a new home they have to have faith in the ability of the agent to find them suitable houses within their price bracket. This truly caring and hardworking man, ensures that the very best options are on offer to all his clients whether they are buying or selling. It was fascinating talking to him and learning a bit more about the intricacies and difficulties that are inherent.

Patrica Lewis and Ann Scholey took the brave step of opening WILLOW in the square just over three and a half years ago; quite an adventure in a time of deep recession. Their instincts were abolutely right however. They felt that a shop which sold quality fabrics and wallpapers togther with well chosen and varied giftware, would do well in Chagford. Over these years Willow has become very well known and todays has overseas customers who send for fabric cuts, which these ladies are only too happy to despatch. One of the secret successes of this business, apart from the cheerful, friendly service, has ben the ability to stock the shop with different and unusual items. Willow specialises in local pottery and crafts. Open six days a week, the shop is closed on Wednesday afternoons.

Something totally different is MARIANNE'S in 6 Mill Street. This is a Delicatessen with a difference. Marianne McCourt who owns it describes the business and herself as being totally crackers! This is a lady who has no hesitancy in bringing the most unusual delicacies into her establishment. It is a bit like a mini Harrod's Food Hall. For all the so called madness, this is a very professionally run business which has grown in stature and brings people to its doors from places well outside Chagford. In addition to the delicatessen, Marianne also runs a very successful Outside Catering operation and will tackle almost any occasion. Whether it is in the shop or for outside, the fare is all home-cooked. Another boon for customers is the home-made frozen ready-made meals. Marianne's is essentially a friendly place and advice is willingly given to anyone who wants or needs it in order to enhance their own entertaining. I wish the business was closer to Plymouth. I do not think I would ever cook again!

Fashion is represented by Chagfords of Chagford which stocks a wide range of famous names and includes shoes by Cheaney. Even the old cinema in an alley behind Steven's Garage has been brought into play. It is now THE CIDER PRESS MUSEUM which houses a unique collection of presses and cider-making equipment from all over Devon, collected by antique dealer, John Meredith, to whose shop in the square you pay the small admission fee.

THE GLOBE INN in the High Street is a popular haunt of locals and visitors. This historic coaching inn is over 200 years old and is full of atmosphere and character, complete with log fires. The two bars and the restaurant offer good food at sensible prices in a relaxing atmosphere. The Globe is recommended in the Good Beer Guide 1994, and you can be certain of a fine selection of well presented Real Ales and other liquid refreshment, all offered at realistic prices. For those who would like to stay there are a limited number of en-suite bedrooms all with colour television, refrigerators and tea and coffee making facilities. This is the sort of inn where you rapidly feel at ease and the locals are more than willing to offer advice and information about this part of Dartmoor and Chagford in particular.

Close by is WHIDDONS ANTIQUES AND TEAROOMS. This is a 16th century building in which 2 rooms are used as tearooms. The room at the rear is in the oldest part of the house and boasts a huge inglenook fireplace. Everything is home-made with a wonderful selection of cakes. The speciality of the house is the Olde English Tea, which comprises cucumber sandwiches, scones, strawberry jam, clotted cream, a slice of cake and a pot of tea. It is delicious. Upstairs are 5 rooms full of antiques of all kinds, bric-a-brac, books and pine furniture.

The 15th and 13th centuries are well represented in the parish church of ST MICHAEL. Mostly 15th century, it has a fine 13th century tower and finely carved roof bosses, some a permanent reminder of the tinner. It is a church that has known drama not the least of which was the murder in 1641 of Mary Whiddon, a daughter of the leading family in Tudor times. She was reputedly shot dead by a jealous lover on leaving the church on her wedding day. The 13th century THREE CROWNS HOTEL is beautiful both inside and out. The striking porch, the uneven floors, the beams, the fires and the hospitality make it a favourite place for regulars and a joyful discovery for those visiting Chagford for the first time. It was at one time the town house of the Whiddon family.

You may soon discover that Chagford and its nearby neighbour Moretonhampstead are not over friendly to each other. During the Civil War, Sidney Godolphin, a Cavalier and poet, met his death in the porch of The Three Crowns during a skirmish with Roundheads from Moretonhampstead. To this day the people of Chagford still refer to Moreton men as 'Roundheads'!

Chagford is a first class base from which to explore many fascinating places and villages within easy distance. The small hamlet of GIDLEIGH is remarkable for two things. Firstly the world renowned GIDLEIGH PARK HOTEL which is the epitome of everything that is excellent in hotelkeeping. Expensive, yes, but to stay here is an experience never to be forgotten. It is a house of grace and elegance where no one is under any pressure to do anything but enjoy the ambience, the superb service, wonderful food and a cellar second to none.

The second is INSIGHT, housed in Gidleigh Studio. Brian Skilton, a producer/director/ cameraman and his partner Deidre Skilton the production manager, restored Gidleigh Mill, created a large pond and restored an old threshing barn and round house for film production offices. Alan van der Steen, a local architect, won the Arnold Sayer award for Gidleigh Mill.

Their independent production company, Insight Productions, was established in 1982. Since then they have produced 39 programmes for British Television, principally for Channel 4. These included arts and entertainment programmes, a feature film, 'Playing Away', a musical drama, 'What a Way to Run a Revolution', staged at the Young Vic theatre and then adapted for television, and the landscape/adventure film, 'Lost Japan' - a journey to the Sacred Mountains.

For the last seven years Brian Skilton has specialised in environmental documentaries. Their book and Video ' Dartmoor the Threatened Wilderness', available from all good bookshops should be compulsory reading for those who love and want to continue exploring the Moor. 'Taming the Flood', 'Camarque', 'New Forest', Naturelands and 'Flavio the Sculptor Who is Blind', have all won acclaim for this enterprising and talented couple .

Brian and Deidre keep Grey Face Dartmoor sheep and spend their free time creating a cottage garden, and managing their 13 acres as a nature reserve. A thoroughly enjoyable, hard working life for them, and a most unusual and unlikely place in which to find a production company.

If you are looking for somewhere to stay I can wholeheartedly recommend GREAT TREE HOTEL at Sandy Park, just outside Chagford. It stands on a south-facing hillside in eighteen acres of its own ground looking out across wooded valleys to the uplands of Dartmoor beyond. Here, sitting in the garden during the summer, or in the lounge by the log fire in winter, one can watch the buzzards soar effortlessly over the hills and woods and hear nothing more than the song of the birds. In the woods surrounding the hotel it is possible to catch a glimpse of the deer, a fox or a badger. Owls doze the day away under the cover of the ivy-clad ancient trees and often a heron can be seen, standing sentinel-like beside the quieter stretches of the stream where it has slowed after its mad rush down the steep hillside.

Great Tree was originally a hunting lodge and has been altered only slightly over the years, so that it still retains its old rather 'Colonial' character whilst providing the comfort and amenities that we all demand today. The entrance hall is a fitting memorial to the marvellous skills of bygone craftsmen, with its ornate fireplace and beautifully carved wooden stairway.

You do not have to be a resident to enjoy the excellence of the food. The menu is changed daily and in his kitchen, Luigi creates and prepares each dish himself using only the freshest and finest ingredients frequently using vegetables from the hotel's own gardens. This is a man who has made cooking his life, perfected it into an art form and the greatest satisfaction he gets is the pleasure watching diners enjoy their meal. It would be hard to find a nicer spot for a romantic evening meal or a weekend away. The ensuite bedrooms are beautifully appointed. The owners, Beverley and Nigel Eaton-Gray are always ready to discuss anything special you may require and they. and their friendly staff, work very hard to make sure that a visit to The Great Tree Hotel is memorable.

THE GREAT TREE HOTEL

There is a delightful pub THE SANDY PARK INN which should be included in your travels. Built 400 years ago of granite cobb, it is thatched and a fine example of a true Devon country inn. Since Richard Holmes became the landlord, he has completely transformed The Sandy Park but in such a manner that not one iota of its character and ambience has been lost. The welcoming bars are devoid of jukeboxes and there are no Pool tables. Three Real Ales are always available and the selection of wines is ever changing, usually at the whim of mine host but always acceptable and at sensible prices. Richard is also the chef and on occasions ably assisted by Jim Coyne who can also be met in his working day role as Curator of FINCH FOUNDRY, a fascinating place, at STICKLEPATH. At lunchtime there is a limited blackboard menu but always good home-made soup, pate, croissants, Pasta dishes and usually Mussels in Devon Cider. In the evening the dishes on offer include succulent steaks, delicious casseroles and fresh salmon and trout.

THE SANDY PARK INN

Close to Sandy Park and just one and a half miles from Whiddon Down is somewhere that I think everyone should visit; STONE LANE GARDENS, complete with THE MYTHIC GARDEN Sculpture Exhibition. Owned by two innovative and far seeing people, Kenneth and June Ashburner, this is a place that fascinates, educates and delights the eye. The whole is part of Stone Farm with a magnificent backdrop of North East Dartmoor. It is an informally landscaped setting for an arboretum of grouped birch and alder grown from wild collected seed. This unique specialist collection from around the northern hemisphere was formed primarily for scientific interest and to make possible the comparison of different species and provenances - testing them against existing classification. Happily this has resulted in a garden in unusual accord with its surrounding countryside.

The landscaping includes streams and ponds with varied and interesting planting, intentionally restrained and relating to the local flora. The romantic appearance of the birch and alder copses and the unobtrusive unity of the five acres make the arboretum an ideal setting for sculpture and the representatin of myth in many media. Magical hidden corners and quiet reflections give confident individuality to varied work by sculptors and designers.

This is a garden which is lovely in all seasons because of the emphasis on positive tree shapes, with subtly different bark colours and framed views between. Many of the incidental plants have also been grown from seed collected on Kenneth Ashburner's botanical expeditions - they have been deliberately massed and repeated in the garden. The arboretum makes concentrated and considered use of a limited range of thoughtfully selected and associated plants. The Ashburners have applied to have the arboretum listed as a National Collection of Birch and Alder Where does the Mythic Garden Sculpture Exhibition fit in? Perhaps I should explain that this is where work by sculptors and designers inspired by Nature, Myth and Folklore are encouraged to display their work in a setting of water gardens and groves of wild origin Birch Alder, in other words within the Arboretum but it is more than that and put quite beautifully in the guide to Stone Lane. For that reason I am taking the liberty of using Alan Lee's own introduction. Firstly he quotes from the 'Epic of Gilgamsesh, Mesopotamia C2,500B.C.

'So Gilgamesh travelled over the wilderness,
he wandered over the grasslands, a long journey, in search of Utnapishtim, whom the gods took after the deluge; and they sent him to live in the land of Dilmun, in the Garden of the Sun; and to him alone of men they gave everlasting life.'

MYTHIC GARDEN

And he continues 'The Hidden Garden, where the fruit or flower of immortality, enlightenment, or some other great gift may be found is a symbol which recurs frequently in religion and myth. The Paradises of the middle and far east, the Garden of the Hesperides on the edge of the western world, the Orchard of Idun in Asgard, Avalon and the numerous otherworld islands of Celtic myth all offer or represent an opportunity to obtain eternal life or reunion with the godhead.

The allegorical gardens of Courtly Romance, the secret walled gardens of fairy tale and the mazes, knot gardens and grottoes which have been incorporated into garden design all attest to the power and longevity of this idea.

The search for these earthly paradises involves long and hazardous journeys, and their guardians are monsters, dragons and angels with flaming swords. Human imagination has created an array of gods, fairies and magical animals to aid or hinder us in our search, though it is what we learn about ourselves through encountering these archetypes that is often the real prize of our quest.

'The Mythic Garden' is an attempt to invest the experience of sculpture, much of it site-specific and temporary - or illusory - in nature, with something of the pattern and spirit of a quest'. When you know that June Ashburner is a painter and the former owner and manager of Chagford Galleries, now using her many years of expertise in organising art exhibitions to create the annual summer sculpture displays at Stone Lane Gardens, then it becomes apparent why The Mythic Garden is so special and different. It is open all the year round by appointment.

The combination of June's talent with those of her husband, Kenneth who is an established expert on birch and alder trees, having travelled throughout the world to collect seeds for Stone Lane Gardens, and is also a landscape designer, gardener, journalist, lecturer and an almost pro jazz musician, is irresistible and demands a visit here to see their creation.

From Chagford there is a delightful circular walk which will take you across ancient bridges, pretty hamlets, and to the charming village of THROWLEIGH, (pronounced 'Ow' as in cow!). Unbothered by time,it has a beautiful village cross, a church with a thatched lychgate and an ancient thatched church house surrounded by other attractive cottages. If you want somewhere to stay 'en famille' where you and your Wellies are very welcome then the Grade II medieval Dartmoor Longhouse, WELL FARM is ideal. It is inexpensive, and an evening meal is available, the bedrooms are ensuite and there is also a ground floor flat.

Between Chagford and Drewsteignton, signposted off the A382 is the famous SPINSTER'S ROCK so called because legend has it that it was built by three spinsters before breakfast! In fact, as I have written in a previous chapter, it is a Neolithic burial chamber, the only one left standing in Devon. Nearby is the setting for a remarkable annual production by the GOLIARDS, a theatre group which includes professionals amongst its members. They perform in an open air setting in the courtyard of a typical thatched Devon farmhouse and for a few days in August a professional performance is staged - from Shakespeare to specially written plays. For dates and times you will need to enquire locally.

Other events in Chagford are the FLEA MARKET every Friday in the Jubilee Hall from 10am-1pm. The local stallholders offer secondhand items or home grown, home-made goods and produce. August is the time of the annual Carnival which is good fun and the Chagford Show is held in the middle of August. That is a truly memorable day out.

FERNWORTHY RESERVOIR is another interesting place to visit. It was built between 1936 and 1942 in order to alleviate some of the summer water problems experienced in Torquay during the tourist season. The Fernworthy Forest, however was first planted in 1921 by the Duchy of Cornwall and it is very pleasurable to stroll along the well-marked forest trail which offers superb views of the moorland, forest and reservoir. The trail is about 4 miles long but if that is too much for you there are several short cuts.

The more I know of Chagford and all that surrounds it, the more I want to go back. It would surprise me if anyone would not enjoy it.

CHAPTER FIVE - CHAGFORD & SURROUNDING VILLAGES

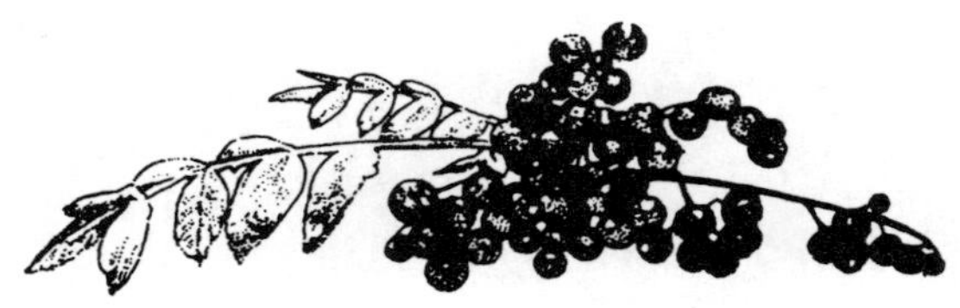

Moretonhampstead owes much of its prosperity over the centuries because of its situation. It lies at the junction of two roads; the B3212 from Exeter across the moor to Yelverton and the A328 from Newton Abbot to Okehampton. Mor Tun, as it was in Saxon times dates from about AD700. It appears in the Domesday Book as Mortona. It is only in recent times that Hampstead was added to the Moreton, and you will find that most locals refer to it still as just Moreton. There can be no doubt that the town owes its development and prosperity to its position on the crossing of what would then have been tracks across the Moor.

Fairs and Markets flourished as various trades developed, especially the woollen industry. Fairs, as well as being important to trade were a source of entertainment. Wrestling was particularly popular and for some reason the men of Moretonhampstead were renowned for their prowess in this tough sport. In 1866 the town became the terminal for the railway line from Newton Abbot. No doubt useful but because farmers and tradesmen found Newton Abbot easily accessible and the markets more affluent, the fairs and local markets slowly declined, and the market ceased altogether in 1918.

Within my lifetime the town has changed considerably. Forty years ago it was a shopping centre for farmers and people living in outlying hamlets. It had everything that a community needed. Today the butcher is still there and the chemist, but the general store is no more and it is only recently that a baker has returned. It gets its livelihood mainly from tourists

The 15th century church of St Andrew, standing on high ground, has tombstones in the porch in memory of two French officers who lived in Moreton during the Napoleonic Wars, when they were on parole from their prison in Princetown.

What an extraordinary race we are! Given half a chance the French would have invaded and made Britain hell had they succeeded and yet we let prisoners wander at large. I wondered who paid for them and where their spending money came from. Do you think we were daft enough to provide that as well? Were they persona grata at social occasions or were society matrons warned to lock up their daughters?

Four major fires occurred between 1845 and 1892 and many of the old buildings were destroyed. Apart from the alms-houses, which were built in 1637 and narrowly missing demolition in the 1930s because they were not considered hygienic, the most stunning building, and the oldest, is MEARSDEN MANOR GALLERY in West Street; I pinched myself to make sure I was awake. It is absolutely full of the most beautiful objects that have been imported from Turkey, Thailand and China.

Large as life statues, carved in wood or cast in bronze, of animals and humans marry up with enormous copper containers catching the light. Turkish carpets are arrayed in all the glory of their rich colours. The jewellery room is full of necklaces, bangles, earrings, lapis and jade, whilst the walls are hung with original paintings and carved wood mirror frames. There are cabinets full of exquisite jade and one of the best collections of Chinese jade carvings and painted ceramics to be found in the country.

Much of the stock brought into the country in container loads is sold on to other establishments because the wholesale trade is a major part of Mearsden's business. I am glad that this does not deprive the Gallery of its lovely things. The criteria for what is bought is that it must be hand-made, of high quality and a sensible price.

Attached to the Gallery is a delightful, oak panelled tea room where you can get a light lunch or enjoy a piece of home-made cake with a piping hot cup of freshly brewed coffee or tea.

Right in the middle of Moreton is the 16th century WHITE HART HOTEL. Once a posting inn where the London-Plymouth coaches pulled in and gave their weary passengers a chance to get refreshment. They would have found, much as we do today, two bars, both warm and friendly. The public bar has a beamed ceiling and horse brasses, where you sit on old settles. The second bar which is now the lounge is comfortably elegant and used more by visitors and residents than the locals who prefer the chatter and banter to be had in the public bar. There is a dining room in keeping with the age of the pub, and outside a beer garden which has no pretensions, is merely a viewless courtyard, but it has been made to look attractive and is a pleasant place to be on a warm day.

You will find the food wide ranging, with something to suit everyone. It is a homely place to stay with the added benefit of a drying room much used by walkers.

The 17th century WHITE HORSE also offers accommodation - 9 rooms, three of which are ensuite. It is a Free house, very friendly, with a good range of bar snacks. The Sunday roast dinner is a speciality of the house. Three ghosts share the pub with its regulars! No one seems to know their history or their sex but they are deemed friendly!

This area is not a walkers paradise because there is a lack of open moorland but nonetheless there are pleasant walks to the north to the prehistoric hill fort of Cranbrook Castle, and to the south to North Bovey.

One good outing from Moreton is along the B3212 which will take you to THE MINIATURE PONY CENTRE which I would not like you to miss. It is the brainchild of Jane and Tony Dennis, two very exciting people. It all started when Tony retired from racing as a jockey and they decided to move from Dorking to the West Country. He opened a stud farm in the South Hams. In amongst the hunters and Arabs, Tony kept miniature ponies which were his wife's hobby.

After a while they found there was more interest in the miniature than in the stud farm, so with great courage and a certain amount of good fortune, they purchased land from the National Park, just before the law was changed, which would not have allowed the sale. For a year they worked around the clock, landscaping and doing everything to produce a centre in which the public could enjoy these delightful animals and gain a deeper understanding of the working and management of a stud. It took them two years before they were ready to open their gates in 1987.

The climate of Dartmoor is particularly suitable for the breeding of Shetland ponies, with the fresh, clear air and rolling countryside that provides shade and shelter in the form of hedges, trees and stone walls.

There are now around 100 ponies in the stud and they are amongst the very smallest in the world. Such tiny ponies are extremely rare and a large number bred at the stud have been exported. To qualify as a miniature, the pony must be no higher than 34 inches. Most of the ponies here are no taller than 32 inches and some are as tiny as 28 inches.

One question I wanted answered; was it man who, by contrivance, had made the Shetland ponies so small? The Denises were quite adamant that the ponies were not dwarfed by starvation and sparse living conditions but rather it was the small pony who was able to survive this, whereas the larger horses and ponies bred in the mild climate of the West Country, given ample food, do not increase in size at all.

The ponies love human company and they have a wonderful nature, which makes them ideal for the smallest member of the family. Because they are sturdy and strong they are easily ridden and also make excellent driving ponies.

The majority of foals are born in April and May. Once they have been weaned at five months, they are stabled in pairs for company and at the same time they are taught their manners and are halter broken.

There is even a nursery in a large covered barn which everyone can enter, and where you can make friends with baby animals. Rare miniature donkeys can be seen here and they just love someone to make a fuss of them.

It depends on how energetic you feel, when it comes to walking round the grounds. The lower walks will take you round the lakes and down to see the beautiful ornamental birds, whilst the higher walk leads to the goat paddock. if you want to walk further you continue onwards and upwards to the larger paddock where you can enter the fields and mingle with the ponies.

I had a lesson in grazing. It never entered my head that if you let nothing but ponies graze in pasture then the land would become 'horse sick'. To prevent this there is an intermixing with cattle, sheep and goats which keeps the paddocks healthy.

At the end of this delightful visit, I wandered into the restaurant from which there are superb views over the lakes. On a warm day sitting out on the pergola or on the terrace is super, and just the place in which to enjoy a meal, or indulge in a Devonshire cream tea.

One word of warning. Please do not feed the animals. The ponies are very well behaved, but the introduction of food creates jealousies amongst them, and they might bite or kick each other, with you in the middle.

PRINCETOWN is as different from Moretonhampstead as chalk from cheese. Most people associate this quiet place with Dartmoor prison and come to stare at its grey, chilling edifice. Of course it is a magnet for tourists armed with cameras in the hopes of catching sight of a prisoner or two, but Princetown has much more to offer. All about it stands 160 square miles of bleak, forbidding moorland, crowned by rocky and frequently mist covered tors, studded with cairns amd stone circles of the prehistoric tribes we know wandered the area. Nonetheless there is a grandeur, a mystery and a magic about it all. You can walk almost anywherein the wild moorland area, but do take care in winter or bad weather. As well as the military firing ranges, to the south-east, beyond South Hessary Tor and Whiteworks lies Foxtor Mires, a notorious area of bog which has been the death of more than one walker and several escaped prisoners.

The great, forbidding prison was built in 1806 for French prisoners of war who were forced to build their own gaol. It must have been appalling. Even on a summer's day Princetown is never the warmest of places, and in the swirling mists of winter penetrating rain eats into one's very soul, so these poor devils must have hated the guts of every Englishman. Some years later Napoleon's men were joined by hundreds of sailors captured during the bitter war with America in 1812. Since 1850 it has been used for British criminals and it was from then onwards it gained its sinister personality.

Sir Thomas Tyrwhitt, who was Lord Warden of the Stannaries, Secretary of the Duchy of Cornwall and a friend of the Prince of Wales is held reposible for the siting of the prison. He was a man whose name in the words of Arthur Mee 'is inseparable from all the great works in Dartmoor.' You will find a tablet to his memory within the church built by American sailors. Its beautiful East window which lights up the rather grim interior, was the gift of American women in honour of 200 of their men who died here in captivity. Sadly, I understand this little church of St Michael and All Angels is threatened with redundancy because of the cost of repairs. The Tyrwhitt Trails are easily followed around Princetown; you will find a leaflet in the High Moorland Visitor Centre. From that you will learn more of this man who at the end of the 18th century had grand designs to convert large areas of moor into arable farmland. His agricultural dream failed due largely to the harsh environment. But he came up wih schemes to revitalise this moorland community, including the building of the prison.

The happiest place in Princetown is THE PLUME OF FEATHERS where James and Linda Langton have been mine hosts since 1968. James is the son of the man who started the Rock Complex at Yelverton, now operated by James's brother. The Plume came into being in 1785 and was the first building to be erected in Princetown during the reign of George III. Here you will get good company, good ale and super food as well as live entertainment at the weekends. The beamed ceilings are the original and with slate tables, copper lamps and open log burners, the bar is a welcoming and comfortable place to be.

In recent years the front of the pub has been restored to its former glory and at the rear, without detracting in any way from the atmosphere of The Plume, the Langtons have converted land into accommodation. Just across the car park there is a site for dormobiles and tents - the only one on the moor. In a sort of hostel, known as the Alpine Bunkhouse, you can stay in what are effectively two dormitories with ten beds in each, a kitchen, dayroom, toilets, showers and drying room - something you will find essential on Dartmoor. If you prefer something a little more sophisticated there are three letting rooms within The Plume. Children are welcome and a special adventure playground has been designed for them. Dogs are also welcome but you are asked to keep them on a lead and undercontrol - there are sheep in the fields behind the pub. The Plume of Feathers can claim to have just about anything and everything that anyone could want - even a ghost which is seen from time to time flitting through the bar.

This year THE PRINCE OF WALES, a 19th century pub has had a complete facelift. I have not yet been there but friends tell me it is good fun and none of the old atmosphere has been lost. There is no accommodation but it offers a wide range of bar snacks as well as a restaurant menu. It is a 'Letter Box' drop and holds four stamps. Like the Plume it is also reputed to be haunted; this time by the ghost of a former landlord who shot himself.

THE HIGH MOORLAND VISITOR CENTRE opened by the Prince of Wales in 1993 is full of information. Housed in what was originally the Duchy Hotel, built between 1809 and 1810 to serve as quarters for officers who were stationed in Princetown to guard prisoners of war, it has now been converted to provide light, spacious rooms in which one can study and purchase any of the myriad of books available about Dartmoor in every aspect. You can enjoy and discover, listen, touch and watch exhibitions of all kinds. You can help build a Dartmoor archive with your impressions, do brass rubbings, and try on a mask to become a Dartmoor legend. The Centre features life-size characters (including Sherlock Holmes),interactive computers, paintings, models, sound and audio-visual programmes and stunning photographic images.

The exciting displays give a unique insight into the natural and cultural heritage of Dartmoor's high moorland. They cover wildlife, archaeology, geology, granite quarrying, peat working, mining, military training, water, farming and forestry, Dartmoor artists and writers, conservation and the story of Princetown itself. The Visitor Centre is a place of discovery in which you can find out how Dartmoor's tors came into being and why Dartmoor looks so different from most other British uplands. It will also tell you what a National Park is and who helps to look after Dartmoor.

There is a delightful range of postcards and of course, free copies of the invaluable Dartmoor Visitor. It has a well informed, friendly and helpful staff who seem to be quite tireless in answering questions. From them you can find out about various events which take place in the Centre including some very good lectures. It is fitting that such a centre should be in the very heart of the Moor.

ST MICHAEL AND ALL ANGELS

MINIATURE PONY

BOVEY TRACEY, the traditional 'Gateway to the Moor' and the home of the Dartmoor National Park Authority, has been important since the days of the Normans, when the manor was held by Edric, a Saxon thane. In the last few years it has lost much of its peacefulness with the arrival of new businesses who have taken the opportunity of entrenching themselves close to the A38. It still has delightful narrow streets and sits sedately on the hillside overlooking the River Bovey. Newcomers may not know some of the wonderful legends that exist about the town and if they did I am not sure they would believe them! Would you believe that Sir William Tracy built the 12th century church of St Thomas a Becket as a penance for being one of his murderers? Not satisfied with one church, he built three.

Sir Williams's church went up in flames 150 years later, but what has been left for us to enjoy, is a 15th century building with a 14th-century tower, which contains some of the finest treasures that Devon has to offer. There is a wealth of carving done almost 600 years ago. The screen has to be one of the finest in the county. Exquisitely carved and decorated with gilded leaves and green grapes, it has 31 Apostles painted on its lower panels. The medieval stone pulpit echoes the carving with more grapes and leaves.

The fine brass lectern brings us to another story. In the 17th century James Forbes was the chaplain to Charles Stuart and also to the forces in the Netherlands and Germany. Having had enough of the hardships and discomfort of this sort of life, he settled down to become vicar of Bovey church, only to find himself ousted by the Puritans. He was able to save the Elizabethan chalice and the registers. Not only that, he preserved the fine brass lectern, which is an eagle with silver claws and three lions at its feet, by throwing it into a nearby pond, praying that a drought would not occur!

With the Restoration and the return of the king, James Forbes set to work to undo all the damage the Puritans had done to his church. The chalice was put back in place, together with the pewter alms dish and flagon which he presented to the church in thanksgiving. Finally the lectern was rescued, all the traces of pond life removed from it. How proud he would be to know that his action saved one of about 50 of these lecterns left in England.

Bovey Bridge was built during the Civil War and herein lies another tale. Royalists occupied Front House when it was attacked by Cromwell. They were playing cards and had not a hope of beating the number of men set against them. With great presence of mind they scattered all the stake money out of the window and whilst the poverty stricken Parliament men scrambled to retrieve the coins, the crafty Royalists escaped unharmed.

There is no doubt that battles were fought at Bovey and Chudleigh Knighton Heath, and it is said that the ghosts of soldiers in Royalists and Cromwellian clothes still haunt the area. Unfinished business do you suppose?

An insight into the craftmanship of the area, both present and past is superbly displayed at Riverside Mill where THE DEVON GUILD OF CRAFTSMEN provide a series of changing exhibitions. Agriculture apart Bovey has seen much development. In the late 18th and 19th centuries the unique Granite tramway carried stone from Haytor quarries bound for Teignmouth docks. It ran through what is now part of STOVER COUNTRY PARK and Templar Way which follows this industrial trail for most of its length.

Bovey clay has special qualities and is in much demand for many industries, especially in the production of fine pottery. Craft pottery in Bovey is represented by the internationally renowned Leach family concerns but until the recent past Bovey Potteries were an essential part of the town from the 19th century.

During the Second World War, Lignite, a fossil fuel, a sort of mixture of peat and coal, was mined in Bovey and the quarry pits, now no longer required have become nature reserves.

The tantalising smell of freshly brewed coffee drew me into THE OLD COTTAGE TEA SHOP in Fore Street where Louise Pawson has been established since 1986. Her reputation for home-made cakes and scones is second to none and would be hard to beat anywhere. You sit in a delightful cottagey atmosphere to enjoy the delicious food on offer. Morning coffee is served between 10am and noon and this is followed by light lunches which begin at twelve and are served until two thirty. The menu is quite extensive and includes a variety of home-made soups and jacket potatoes with a whole range of fillings. Louise is known for the lightness of her omelettes as well as producing some interesting and slightly different salads and sandwiches. Anyone with a sweet tooth will revel in the mouth-watering desserts usually accompanied by Devonshire clotted cream. Disastrous for anyone like myself trying to diet but almost irresistible.

Afternoon tea is yet another temptation. Apart from the scones, cakes, sandwiches and hot and cold snacks, Louise makes the most gorgeous clotted cream filled meringues! Teas are served until 5.30pm.

Bovey has two good pubs which I have enjoyed over the years. THE OLD THATCHED INN is a 17th century Free house, once a coaching inn, with one long bar divided in two by the large chimney in the middle. There are fireplaces on both sides of the chimney. There is a stone floor and low oak beams. The bar food is good, sensibly priced and the house speciality is a flambe menu on offer five days a week in the evenings only.

THE RIVERSIDE INN which has 10 en-suite bedrooms, has the River Bovey running alongside the car park and a stream that trickles through beneath the building. It is a tranquil, charming establishment, much loved by its regular clientele and those who discover it for the first time. I have personal experience of a delightful wedding reception that I attended here. The English and French menu has dishes which will please the most discerning of palates and in the busy bars you will find well kept Real Ales and a regular Guest Bitter. For those who enjoy fishing the Inn has its own rights.

Set in an historic Pottery building is THE HOUSE OF MARBLES AND TEIGN VALLEY GLASS. The whole place is one of enchantment. The Bovey Potteries were here for almost 300 years until 1957 but they have been brought to life again by the present incumbents - Britain's only glass marble manufacturer. A museum depicting the history of the pottery, the history of the glass and the glass marbles is open, free of charge to visitors to the restaurant and for a small fee to others.

The restaurant, aptly named THE POTTERY RESTAURANT retains all the atmosphere of the building's history with many exhibits. The menu is wide ranging with many innovative and exciting dishes. For example, Scrumping Porkers, a dish of pork and orchard apples cooked in a tasty cider and tomato sauce topped with a puff pastry cover - or Gardener's Parcel made up of lots of fresh vegetables from the garden, baked in a pastry case and served with lots of freshly prepared salad. There are delicious desserts, tempting starters and a first class Devonshire Cream Tea. For lovers of tea, the choice is yours from Indian, Assam to Rosehip and Camomile. The Pottery Restaurant without doubt enhances a visit to The House of Marbles and Teign Valley Glass. There are few places with such high standards, generous portions and at the same time inexpensive.

There is a very pleasant walk from Bovey to Parke, where you can see the Rare Breeds Farm, which I have written about in a previous chapter. You will come to the disused railway line and take your time enjoying a truly beautiful circular walk of the Parke Estate, most of it on National Trust land. You can walk on to Houndtor Wood or around Haytor. Just within the Park boundary lies Yarner Wood, a National Nature Reserve which has some fine woodland trails.

From Bovey it is a short drive to WHITSTONE VINEYARDS. You will find it on the right after leaving town on the old A382 just past the turn to Bovey Tracey Hospital. This is an English Vineyard whose wines have won numerous awards. One wine was featured on the BBC Food and Drink Programme. Overlooking Dartmoor, its location is lovely. Wine is for sale Monday-Friday 8am-noon and you are invited to wander through the vineyard and afterwards enjoy a taste of the wines in an attractive tasting room right above the Vineyard. Guided tours are given on all August Tuesdays from 10am-5pm. Group tours can be arranged in advance for any time. The owners, Mr and Mrs Barclay are very friendly and helpful. If you would like to visit outside regular hours do please telephone in advance.

Bovey Tracey is worth exploring as is so much around it. I think if I were staying here I would make sure that a visit to the superb UGBROOKE HOUSE at Chudleigh was included in my itinerary. The home of the Clifford family, it is set in a valley and surrounded by a beautiful landscaped park with two lakes, which were contrived by the inimitable Capability Brown. Inside there are simple Adam interiors but with that well-proportioned, light and airy style that is his hallmark. You will probably be surprised by the ornate chapel which is Italian Renaissance at its best and quite a contrast to its prim Adam front.

The house was built by Thomas Clifford, the favourite of Charles II. A statesman, he is always remembered as one of the five who formed the first of all Cabinets, the Cabal Ministry. He was a brave and valiant soldier, fighting with all his fervour in the war with the Dutch in 1665. It was rumoured that he was a Roman Catholic and under the laws of the land it became impossible for him to remain in office. The strange anomaly is that he built his Protestant chapel in which he is buried but he refused to avow that he was a Protestant or deny that he was a Catholic. What we do know is that his self-enforced retirement from public affairs broke his heart and he hung himself in August 1673 at the age of 43.

Chudleigh's coaching inn once housed William of Orange after he landed at Torbay, and from one of its windows he spoke to the townsfolk. They were gratified, but his English was so bad that it is doubtful if they understood one word of what he had to say.

The motley coloured 14th-century church is worth exploring for its unusual bench ends if nothing else, and not far off is the rewarding sight of a delightful glen from which water cascades onto the rocks beneath. Then there is the unusual Chudleigh Rocks and Pixie's Hole in which prehistoric animal bones and other relics have been found. The walls are covered with initials carved by the youth of the past, including Samuel Taylor Coleridge and his brother. Nothing much changes does it?

Another delightful outing is a day spent at CANONTEIGN FALLS, set in the heart of a private 100 acre site. It is a joy to visit at any season, with its waterfalls, lakes and abundant wildlife. This is Devon at its best - wild, beautiful, unspoilt by the passing of time. the exciting nature trails are about one mile in length and take in the woods, waterfalls and lakes. The trails are steep in places. Buzzard's View, at the top of Lady Exmouth Falls provides one of the most outstanding panoramic rural views in the whole of England. Lady Exmouth Falls has a sheer drop of 220feet, making it the highest in England. Clampitt Falls and the Secret Garden Falls must also be seen. The lakes and ponds provide a natural habitat for waterfowl and water plants - perfect for a peaceful stroll or leisurely picnic.

There can hardly be anyone who would not finding something beautiful to remember here. Families love the carefree, safe terrain with a Play House, a Wendy house and a Junior Commando Assault Course. There are miniature ponies and sheep - you are asked to keep your dog on a lead please! The Nature Interpretation Centre is fascinating and informative and made much use of by schools. One of the latest additions is the super Wildlife and Wetland Nature Reserve. This is a Naturalists and Photographers' paradise. To stroll amidst this unspoilt beauty is unforgettable.

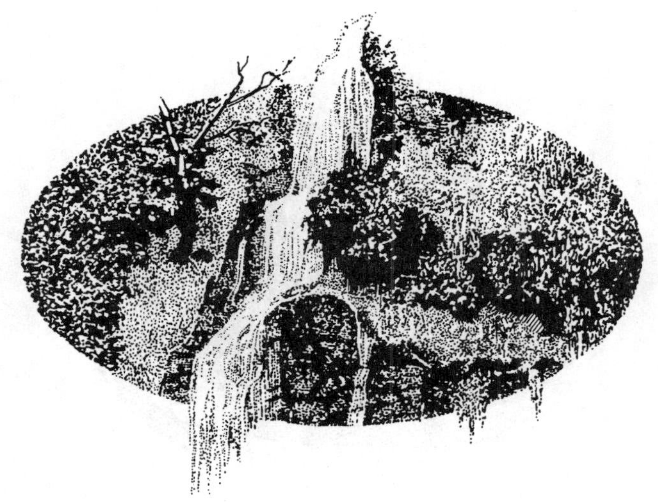

CANONTEIGN FALLS

THE OLD DRINKING FOUNTAIN BOVEY TRACEY

The history of Ashburton might almost be that of any Devonshire market town. It has known times of high prosperity and the other extreme. Today, bypassed by the A38 it is a busy but peaceful little town unbothered by what goes on in the rest of the world. Ashburton took its name from the stream which runs through it, the Ashburn which is now known as the Yeo. A town of contrasts and beauty, it was designated a Stannary town in 1305. During the latter part of the 12th century the tin mining developed enormously and because of Ashburton's position it became a natural collecting centre for the south-eastern side of the Moor. It is the tin mining and the wool industry which brought Ashburton its wealth and with it the building of some fine houses. One in North Street still remains. It was a 17th century gambling house, known as the Card House. You will see the reason why because of the clubs, diamonds, spades and hearts that form the pattern on its slate-hung facade. These slate-hung houses are one of the town's attractions. What is now the ironmongers on the corner of North Street was once the Mermaid inn where the Roundhead, General Fairfax, had his headquarters after defeating the Royalists nearby. That many people were Royalists and were prepared to risk their lives hiding them, is evidenced by the little carvings of a man on horseback on one of the houses - a sign that Royalists were safe there.

The cloth industry ran alongside that of mining, siting the fulling mills on the banks of the Ashburn from which sufficient power was produced to drive the wheels. It was the great increase in road traffic in 1660 which brought more inns and other trades to the town. Ashburton lay conveniently, half way between Plymouth and Exeter. For some time iron-mining was also carried out here. The ruins of one furnace still exists and the old shafts are to be found in the hills immediately above. The 18th century probably saw Ashburton at its zenith. The ending of the East India Company's monopoly of the China trade in 1833 sounded the death knell to Ashburton's trade. The population fell as workers moved away seeking to make a living elsewhere. Then, adding insult to injury, the opening of the South Devon Railway in 1846 bypassed the town by several miles and in so doing took with it most of the coaching and wagon trade.

Ashburton still carries on many old traditions. For example it has a Saxon heritage, a Portreeve. The name comes from 'Port' or market town and 'Reeve', an official. Today the Portreeve is the social head of the town. The role does carry duties. He or she has to join the Leet Jury of Ale testers and Bread Weighers and on one evening is obliged to knock on the door of each public house to try a sample of their beer. It is as well that Ashburton is quite small because there are ten pubs and it would take quite a lot of stamina to visit them all. The Bread Weighers weigh the bread from the baker's shop and providing it is satisfactory, a certificate is given together with a piece of evergreen. The custom now is for the bread to be auctioned at the local recreation ground whilst everyone is enjoying a ram roast. Nine times a year there is a market, one of which, in October, is for the sale of Dartmoor ponies.

THE LONDON HOTEL is a delightful, olde worlde, coaching inn, once much in demand as a staging post for the coaches on the London-Plymouth road. Those days have gone but it is equally in demand as a pub into which the Thompson family, Mimi and Melvyn make you welcome and immediately at ease. It is furnished in a traditional manner with a mixture of old church pews, wheel back chairs and some interesting tables made of cider barrels topped with brass. The added bonus is two splendid real coal fires that warm the cockles of the heart on a cold day. It is very much a haunt of the regulars; always a good sign of a well kept inn, and if you ask them what beer they drink, they will probably tell you 'Thompsons Best Bitter'. Yes, The London Inn has its very own Thompson's Brewery alongside. Good, wholesome, home-made food is available seven days a week, both at lunchtime and in the evening. There are always Blackboard Specials but probably the favourite is a Steak and Kidney Pie full of juicy meat and topped with pastry that melts in the mouth.

A Function suite which will house 100 is a popular venue for local occasions and for wedding receptions, and recently 5 ensuite bedrooms have been opened for those who want to stay and enjoy the fun and comfort of the pub as well as the surrounding countryside.

The 15th-century church tower is beautiful with delightful double buttresses, a charming turret, and over the west door three niches. In the centre is a gentle Nativity scene and at the sides are St Catherine and Thomas a Becket. It is a church full of treasures and one to be savoured. In the churchyard I found a grave of a French officer who had been paroled in Ashburton during the Napoleonic Wars. I had not realised that there were places other than Moretonhampstead where this happened. The grave has an offshoot of the willow growing by Napoleon's grave at St Helena. Planted, so I understand, by a French visitor years later.

Whether to be encouraged to visit THE GOLDEN LION because it is the headquarters of the monster Raving Loony Party, headed by Screaming Lord Sutch, or to stay away because of it, is your decision. If you decide against it,you will be missing an opportunity to visit a place that is out of the ordinary. It is primarily, a thriving market town pub, busy with locals who come in for the fun and the beer. It is however somewhere you can stay if you wish. You will certainly be entertained. Alan Hope and his wife Norma are the landlords and they are both members of the Raving Loony party. In fact Norma seems to be the mainstay of the administration. Alan is a larger than life character who has done more than ruffle the feathers of the more staid Ashburtonians since their arrival fifteen years ago. He was once the leader of a rock and roll group and brings live music to the Golden Lion regularly. If you can get him to talk about his record collection you will discover that he has one of the largest in the South West.

I wondered where Screaming Lord Sutch acquired the money to fight elections and almost always lose his deposit. The telephone rang at least three times whilst I was talking to Alan and Norma and each time it was a newspaper or a magazine wanting to write an article about his lordship for which they were willing to pay; the question was answered. The publications concerned might be a little different from the normal politcal journal, but why not? I am sure Club International and Razzle Magazine will do him proud! The membership of the party is interesting, too. People from all over the world belong.

THE RIVER DART COUNTRY PARK just outside the town on the Two Bridges road must be included in your list of places to see. It is open to everyone who appreciates the pleasures of the countryside. It is a beautiful riverside estate to which has been added all sorts of things to do and see. From the breathtaking Anaconda Run which snakes its way through the undergrowth, guaranteed to excite the most adventurous of children, but not for the faint hearted, Adventure Playgrounds with Tarzan swings, tree houses and rope bridges, to bathing in safety and fun with your own inflatable in the specially formed river fed lake with a hard bottom and a maximum of one metre in depth, it is fun all the way. Then there are woodland walks, pony riding, a picnic meadow and fly fishing for salmon and trout in the Dart, available at reasonable rates. Rods are not provided. The excellent self service cafeteria, bar and tea garden, cater for all tastes. A thoroughly good day out for the whole family.

Ashburton is also close to one of my favourite watering holes, THE HOLNE CHASE HOTEL which is just a little further up the road from The River Dart Country Park, but certainly not somewhere to be missed, even if it is only for a cup of tea.

For horse racing enthusiasts the courses at Newton Abbot and Exeter are within easy distance; both have regular meetings throughout the year. Newton Abbot racecourse also plays host to Stock Car Racing. Greyhound race meetings are held at the Newton Abbot racecourse every Tuesday and Thursday and at the County Ground stadium, Exeter on Wednesdays and Saturdays. The town is also well sited for exploring Devon. It is only 8 miles or so from Torquay, Paignton, Babbacombe, Teignmouth and many other superb beaches. Dartmoor is on the doorstep with its matchless beauty.

BUCKFASTLEIGH, just south of Ashburton, is a charming place of narrow streets set between the River Dart, the Mardle, Holy Brook and the Dean Burn, which flow from Dartmoor. It has grace and a character of its own, although it is often overshadowed by BUCKFAST ABBEY, a little way up the road. I found a friendly welcome at THE WATERMAN'S ARMS in Chapel Street which opens all day, six days a week, has inexpensive bed and breakfast accommodation and provides good, traditional home-made pub fare as well as Real Ales.

Seldom have I seen or heard anything quite so dramatic as Buckfast Abbey at night during the service of Compline. The monks come silently down the aisle, the only sound the swish of their long robes as they pass by, the only light a bidding one high over the altar. As they reach their stalls, they push back the cowls from their heads and the service starts. Its simple message is chanted and reaches out to every corner of this great building. One cannot doubt that God is present.

The most impressive thing about Buckfast is that the present abbey was rebuilt by just four monks, who at the outset had no experience of this sort of work at all. They just used commonsense and dogged determination, coupled with the sure knowledge that God was with them. One of these monks is still alive and living at the abbey.

The first monastery was founded in AD 1018, in the reign of Cnut. In 1147 the abbey was rebuilt and transferred to the Cistercian order. After the Dissolution on 25 February, 1539, years of decline and dereliction followed, until the complete restoration of the monastery by this small group of Benedictine monks. Work began in January 1907, based upon the original Cistercian foundations and the final church stone was laid in July 1937.

The exterior walls of the church and domestic buildings were built of local blue limestone. The window arches, quoins, coping stones and turrets of the tower are in mellow Ham Hill stone, a little softer than the limestone.

Dedicated to the Virgin Mary, the Lady Chapel has some of the most amazing marble mosaics, using marble taken from the ancient Greek and Roman buildings. the marble floor depicts the biblical Tree of Jesse, symbolising Christ's descent from David and his father Jesse,and was made in the abbey's own workshop. There are four ambulatory chapels, the Chapel of the Blessed Sacrament gives a modern touch to the abbey, and is a place of quiet prayer for the monks and visitors. The astonishing colour of the glass in the windows almost distracts one from prayer. The incoming light reflects above the High Altar producing a stunning effect.

The Chapel of St Benedict is dedicated to the father of western monasticism. Born as a Roman aristocrat in AD480, Benedict decided to live life as a hermit and later wrote his rules for monks, which is as valid today as it was over 1,500 years ago.

Monasteries need to be self-sufficient to survive as they are not funded by churches or the state. They are like a huge family rallying around to support each other and the communities' older generations. In the Middle Ages, Buckfast gained much of its income from the wool trade. Today a farm is run by the Brothers and is better known for its honey and tonic wine than its wool.

It has been difficult for the monks here living within the Benedictine rules which made it quite possible for them to be sent to other monasteries. This caused problems, when loss of experienced and trained monks from their duties at Buckfast, held up essential work. Now when someone joins the community he becomes a Buckfast Benedictine and does not move.

Bees have always been kept at Buckfast Abbey. Brother Adam who was head beekeeper for over 70 years developed a new bee known as the Buckfast bee, and gained recognition world wide, and an OBE. The queens are held in isolation in Dartmoor but have 320 hives in the abbey grounds, local farms and orchards. Together with the honey that has become famous, so too has the wine made in the monastery cellars. Buckfast tonic wine is sold all over the world.

Buckfast was not always as relaxed and until the 1940's was one of the strictest communities. They were only allowed to talk for an hour a day and sign language was used at all other times. They even had to kneel when speaking to the Abbot. During World War II Buckfast became a fire station and outside influences crept in.

There are many things to see, and if you are male, no better way to witness the life of a monk than to take on that role; not in any permanent way but as one of the 250 retreatants who come to Buckfast to stay usually three or four nights. All walks of life enter this calm and peaceful retreat, among them writers, accountants and students doing their A levels; all looking for rest or spiritual enlightenment. There is no charge but the guests are invited to contribute.

When you go to see the Abbey allow sufficient time to sit awhile and drink in the beauty of this astonishing building. Look up to the roof and see the magnificent paintings. Read the various pieces of history that are laid out for you. Take note of the little balconies from which sick monks can take a part in a service even if they are bedridden.

You will always find one or more of the monks in the abbey who are more than happy to tell you about its history and their work.

An unusual sight in the grounds is the presence of a small Methodist chapel. Seldom used for services, its doors are always open for anyone wishing to go in. I am told that the offertory here is frequently greater than that of the nearest operational Methodist place of worship! I am not quite sure how it got there.

Sadly the old 13th and 15th century parish church of Buckfastleigh was the subject of the attention of arsonists two years ago and totally destroyed. A decision has yet to be made about its rebuilding. I hope it will be. The ruins stand high above the little town looking down on the abbey, forlorn and just waiting to be given new life.

The little station at Buckfastleigh is the home of SOUTH DEVON STEAM RAILWAY which operates between here and Littleham just outside Totnes throughout the summer months and at weekends sometimes in the winter. It is a delightful train journey running alongside the River Dart, amidst lush fields and pretty woodlands. Frequently there are special train and steam days. Thomas Tank is always popular and so are the Christmas journeys with Santa aboard. You can have a truly wonderful day out here with a ride on the train and then with children, if you have any, off to the ten acres of riverside grounds that form a leisure park, workshops where engines undergo repair, a small museum and THE BUTTERLY CENTRE. There is also a fascinating OTTER SANCTUARY closeby.

Another good outing is THE PENNYWELL SOUTH DEVON FARM CENTRE. It is only one and a half miles down the road from Lower Dean, so if you are coming from Plymouth or Exeter watch out for the Lower Dean exit on the A38.

The husband and wife team, the Murrays are dedicated to organic farming and have achieved enormously high standards, winning themselves some prestigious awards en route. Make sure you take your camera when you visit here. It will provide you with a record of one of the happiest and most instructive days out that you could wish for. You have the added bonus of wonderful countryside overlooking the Dart valley to top it.

There is no doubt that animals and plants thrive on this chemically free environment. You can try your hand at milking a cow or goat, feed the poultry, pick up free range eggs or wander along the farm trail. The Murrays have thought it out so splendidly that you will find there is always some other activity in which you can take part when you have completed another. My grandchildren think it is the greatest place ever, particularly when they are allowed to ride on the play tractor.

I listened to people asking endless questions which were all answered with enthusiasm and total patience. Things like how much does it cost to rear a piglet. Or do chickens really produce 250 eggs a year. Children and adults are encouraged to cuddle a calf, pick up a piglet or any other animal for that matter. There are no restrictions, you can wander anywhere. All that is asked of you is to obey the Country Code and use commonsense.

At the end of your visit if you are a trifle weary you can sit down and have what is known as a Pennywell snackette or a super Devonshire tea in the attractive cafe. A wonderful outing to finish my Dartmoor trail

SOUTH DEVON STEAM RAILWAY

GOLDEN LION, ASHBURTON

A-Z

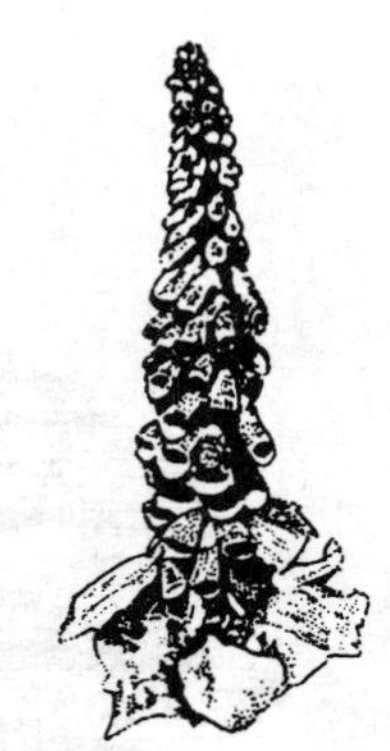

D

E

F

G

H

T

U

V

W

THE OLD POTTERY RESTAURANT
BOVEY TRACEY

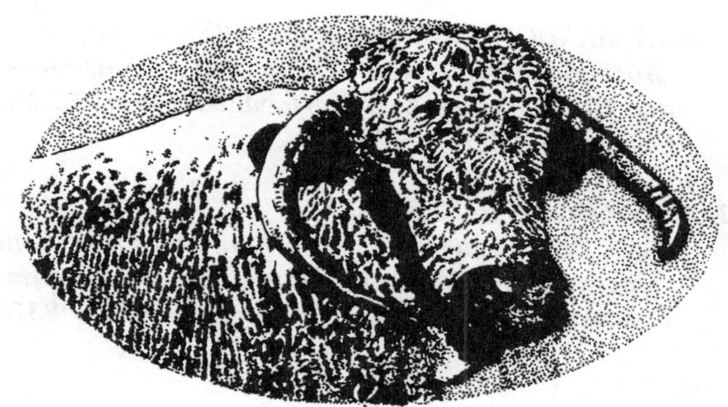

LONG HORNED BULL

A GUIDE TO CAMPING AND CARAVANNING ON DARTMOOR AND WHERE TO BUY YOUR EQUIPMENT

The list below is compiled of many, easily accessible sites. You are asked to use sites rather than pull off the road for an overnight stop. Apart from spoiling the view and polluting the streams, the very things you have come to enjoy, you will be committing an offence against local byelaws. The maximum penalty is one hundred pounds and you may find yourselves being moved on by Police or Rangers just as you have settled down for the night. Do remember that many Dartmoor roads are steep and winding and really not suitable for towing a caravan or trailer. In fact caravans are banned entirely from crossing Holne Bridge and New Bridge. Both are on the road from Ashburton to Two Bridges. The National Park is there for you to enjoy and this enjoyment will be enhanced if you leave your caravan on a site on the edge of the moor and explore without it.

1. *ASHBURTON CARAVAN PARK,*
   Waterleat, Ashburton. 40 pitches for tents and motor homes in scenic valley. Superb facilities. Highly recommended. Open Easter to early October. Tel: 0364 652552

2. *BARLEY MEADOW CARAVAN & CAMPING PARK,*
   Crockernwell, Nr. Exeter. Quiet. 30 caravan/motor home and 10 tent pitches. Excellent facilities. Open 15th March to October. Tel: 0647 21629

3. *BRIDESTOWE CARAVAN PARK,*
   Glebe Park, Bridestowe, Nr Okehampton. Quiet, family run park on edge of Dartmoor for touring caravans, tents, motor caravans. ETB 'very good' grading. Tel: 083786 261

4. *CHESTON CARAVAN PARK,*
   Folly Cross, South Brent. Immaculately maintained site with all facilities. Barbecue area. Playground. Tel: 0364 72586

5. CLIFFORD BRIDGE PARK,

Clifford, Nr. Drewsteignton. 20 pitches for caravans and 45 for tents. Heated swimming pool. Open Easter to end of September. Tel: 0647 24226

6. COCKINGFORD CAMPSITE,

Cockingford Farm, Widecombe-in-the-Moor. 30 sites for caravans/motor homes. 30 sites for tents. Open 15th March-15th November. Tel: 03642 258.

7. CULVERHAYES CARAVAN AND CAMPING PARK,

Culverhayes, Sampford Courtenay, Nr Okehampton. Some hard standings on a gently sloping site. Permanent sites available for tourers. Open mid March- end October. Tel: 0837 82431

8. DARTMOOR VIEW CARAVAN PARK,

Whiddon Down, Okehampton. Tourers and tents welcome. ETB excellent grading. All facilities. Open 15th March-15th November. Tel: 0647 231545.

9. FINLAKE LEISURE PARK,

Chudleigh, Nr Newton Abbot. 130 acre site combining a lively holiday complex with acres of quiet woodland. 450 touring caravans & camping pitches. Indoor pool and entertainment. Tel: 0626 853833

10.HARFORD BRIDGE PARK,

Peter Tavy, Tavistock. Beautiful flat sheltered park within Dartmoor. River Tavy borders the park providing super riverside camping. Tel: 0822 810349

11. HIGHER LONGFORD FARM,

Moorshop, Tavistock. Small, friendly. Level sheltered pitches with outstanding views of the moor. Tel: 0822 613360

12. LANGSTONE MANOR CARAVAN & CAMPING PARK,

Langstone Manor, Moortown, Tavistock. Family run site covering 5 acres of mature grounds. In Dartmoor National Park at foot of Pew Tor. Open 15th March-15th November. Tel: 0822 613371.

13. LEMONFORD CARAVAN PARK,

Bickington, Newton Abbot. One of the prettiest parks in

South Devon. Rose Award 1993, AA award 1992. Excellent facilities for tourers and tents. Open Easter to end September. Tel: 0626 821242.

14. *LOWER ASH GUEST HOUSE & CAMPING SITE,*
Poundsgate, Nr. Ashburton. 15 sites for caravans/motor homes/ tents. Open March to November. Tel: 03643 229.

15. *DARTMOOR COUNTRY HOLIDAYS MAGPIE LEISURE PARK,*
Bedford Bridge, Horrabridge, Yelverton. Beautiful woodland site beside banks of the river Walkham on the edge of the National park. 30 pitches for caravans/tents. New toilet block & launderette. Tel: 0822 852651.

16. *OLDITCH CARAVAN AND CAMPING PARK,*
Sticklepath, Okehampton. Small, quiet, family run. Direct access to Dartmoor. Pitches for tourers/motor homes/ tents. Modern toilet block, free showers. Licensed restaurant. Tel: 0837 840734.

17. *PLUME OF FEATHERS CAMPSITE,*
Princetown. 6 sites for motor caravans and 75 for tents. Open all year. Adventure playground. Site is directly behind Plume of Feathers Inn. Tel: 0822 890240.

18. *PREWLEY CARAVAN PARK,*
Sourton Cross, Okehampton. Nice surroundings, pleasant views. On main A30 Cornwall road. Open March to November. Tel: 0837 86611.

19. *SPRINGFIELD HOLIDAY PARK,*
Tedburn Road,, Tedburn St Mary, Exeter. 'Excellent' graded park. Rose award 1994. AA campsite of the year 1993. Beautiful views, level pitches set in 9 acres. Super place. Dogs welcome. Open March to October. Tel: 0647 24242.

20. *STOVER INTERNATIONAL CARAVAN PARK,*
Lower Staplehill, Newton Abbot. beautifully landscaped park with sites for caravans/motor homes/tents. Exceptionally well kept and spotlessly clean. Heated indoor swimming pool. One night halts except July and August. Open 15th March to end October. Tel: 0626 821446.

21. THE RIVER DART COUNTRY PARK LIMITED,
Holne Park, Ashburton. Top quality camping/caravanning park set in beautiful 90 acre Victorian Country estate, alongside River Dart. Also children's woodland adventure playgrounds for non-stop activity. Open April-September. Tel: 0364 652511.

22. WEBLAND FARM HOLIDAY PARK,
Avonwick, South Brent. Enchanting park with magnificent views over Dartmoor. Low density five acre park with acres of space for children to play in complete safety. Open March to November. Tel: 0364 73273.

23. WHITE OAKS OF IVYBRIDGE,
David's Lane, Davey's Cross, Filham, Ivybridge. Quiet, level site just off A38 on moor's edge with panoramic views of the South Hams. 24 caravan/motor home/tents. Takeaway meal service. Booking advisable in high season. Open to March to October. Tel: 0752 892340.

24. WOODOVIS HOLIDAY PARK,
Tavistock. Quiet, sheltered park. 54 pitches for touring caravans, tents & motor homes. Heated indoor swimming pool. AA award for environmental excellence. Open March-December. Tel: 0822 832968

25. YERTIZ CARAVAN AND CAMPING PARK,
Exeter Road, Okehampton. Small, friendly site for caravans/motor homes/tents. Open all year. Tel: 0837 52281.

WHERE TO BUY YOUR CAMPING AND OUTDOOR KIT

CAMPING AND OUTDOOR CENTRE - ROYAL PARADE, PLYMOUTH Tel: 0752 662614

The Camping and Outdoor Centre in Royal Parade, Plymouth is part of the retail division of Scout Shops Ltd, who opened their first shop supplying outdoor clothing and equipment in 1917.

The company slogan is Quality, Advice and Service, which is interpreted as top brand name products, great value prices, and staff who are trained and keen to please. In Plymouth as well as the official company outdoor training, the staff treat Dartmoor as their own personal training ground. They also participate in that unique Dartmoor pursuit letterboxing. The shop has its own letter box stamp, half of which is on the moor and the other half in the special Dartmoor map and guide department in the shop.

The shop caters very much for walking on Dartmoor, or elsewhere for that matter, with its large range of walking boots and accessories, plus outdoor clothing such as waterproofs and fleece with a separate section for Barbour. There is also a large tent showroom with tents for family, touring and lightweight camping, and everything you need to enjoy the outdoor life, including of course rucsacs and sleeping bags.

As well as the Scout Association which benefits from its profits, the company has links with many other outdoor bodies. For instance you can join the Y.H.A at the shop, or collect application forms to join the Ramblers Association or the Camping and Caravanning club.

BOWDEN SPORTS, 51 Mayflower Street, Plymouth, Tel: 0752 663566,

... offers equipment for whatever sport you follow. They are stockists of leading names in Footwear, Rucksacks and Waterproofs. A helpful, well informed staff are endlessly patient in making sure your equipment is right for you.

TAUNTON LEISURE

- inside any one of the Taunton Leisure Stores you will find all the equipment necessary to suit your Outdoor and Leisure needs! A FREE COLOUR MAIL ORDER CATALOGUE is available. Tel: 0823 331875 for details. The stores are situated at 40, East Reach Taunton, Tel: 0823

331875, 72 Bedminster Parade, Bedminster, Bristol, Tel: 0272 637640, 206 High Street, Swansea Tel: 0792 476515, 110 Fore Street, Exeter, Tel: 0392 410534, 1045 Stratford Road, Hall Green, Birmingham, Tel: 021 777 3337.

BRASHER BOOT COMPANY LIMITED

... invite you to discover Dartmoor's National Park with happier feet, wearing Britain's classic lightweight leather walking boots. The famous Hillmaster Classic and the Hillmaster GTX, with its unique use of Gore-Tex, are now both available in womens' fittings. Available from James Bowden, Chagford 0647 433272, Moorland Rambler, Exeter 0392 431006, Percy Hodge, Newton Abbot 0626 54923, Kountry Kit, Tavistock, 0822 613089, Bowden Sports, Plymouth, 0752 663566 & Barrons 0752 255661. For Nationwide Stockists Tel: 0524 841000.

CALOR GAS STOCKISTS IN DEVON

EXETER	*Exeter Calor Centre, Grace Road, Marsh Barton Trading Estate - Tel: 0392 54959*
HOLSWORTHY	*Don Jefferies Ltd, 1 Fry Street Tel: 0409 253569*
LAUNCESTON	*Don Jefferies Ltd, Newport Ind Est. Tel: 0566 772579*
PLYMOUTH	*Plymouth Calor Centre, Tel: 0752 664184*
TAVISTOCK	*Calor Gas Centre, Wilminstone Ind Est, Old Exeter Road - Tel: 0822 615451*

There are over 100 Calor Stockists in Devon so please contact one of the dealers listed above for your nearest supplier.

OUT AND ABOUT WITH PUBLIC TRANSPORT AND INFORMATION CENTRES

ASHBURTON:

X39 from Exeter and Plymouth, 88 from Newton Abbot and Buckfastleigh, Daily. 672 from Buckland in the Moor and Widecombe Less than daily. Pannier market Tuesday mornings, Early closing Wednesday.

BECKY FALLS;

671 from Whiddon Down. Less than daily. 171 from Newton Abbot. Summer months only. No admission charge for bus passengers.

BOVEY TRACEY:

X39 from Exeter and Plymouth. 73/173 from Newton Abbot and Moretonhampstead. 72 from Newton Abbot. Daily. 671 from Whiddon Down. Less than daily. 170/171 Newton Abbot Circular 173 Okehampton and Moretonhampstead. Summer months only.

BUCKFASTLEIGH:

X39 from Exeter and Plymouth. 88 from Newton Abbot. 165 from Totnes. Daily. 893 from Holne.Less than daily. South Devon Railway from Totnes. Summer months only.

BUCKFAST ABBEY;

X39 from Exeter and Plymouth (ask the driver to stop as near to the junction for the Abbey, then follow signs on foot) 88 from Newton Abbot.Daily. 893 from Holne.Less than daily. Free admission except exhibition.

BUCKFAST BUTTERFLY FARM
& DARTMOOR OTTER SANCTUARY

Any bus or train to Buckfastleigh. The complex is adjacent to the South Devon Railway

BUCKLAND ABBEY:

55 from Yelverton (connects with 83/84 service from Plymouth & Tavistock). Daily. Admission charge.

BURRATOR RESERVOIR:

48 from Plymouth. Less than daily

BUS WALKS IN WEST DEVON

In West Devon you can enjoy an enchanting part of the Devon countryside without taking your car. For more information, look out for the West Devon Bus Walks leaflet or ring (0822) 615911.

CANONTEIGN FALLS;

887 from Newton Abbot (ask the driver to stop at the turning for Canonteign Falls on the B3193, then walk uphill for approx a quarter of a mile. Less than daily

CASTLE DROGO;

359 from Exeter & Moretonhampstead. Daily. 174 Okehampton & Moretonhampstead. Summer service only. National Trust. Admission charge

CHAGFORD:

359 from Exeter. Daily. 860 from Moretonhampstead. 671 from Whiddon Down. Less than daily. 174 from Okehampton & Moretonhampstead. Summer service only.

CHUDLEIGH:

X39 from Exeter & Plymouth 72/83 from Newton Abbot Daily.

DARTINGTON CIDER PRESS,DARTINGTON;

X80 from Plymouth & Torquay. 165 from Totnes & Buckfastleigh (both to Shinners Bridge). Daily. X64 from Kingsbridge. Less than daily. Free admission.

DARTMEET:

Meeting point East and West Dart Rivers. See Dartmoor Public Transport Guide for details of summer services.

DARTMOOR:

82 Transmoor Link. See Dartmoor from the Top Deck Panoramic views, stunning moorland scenery. Runs across Dartmoor between Plymouth and Exeter. Get off wherever you like. Service runs May to September (daily in high summer).

DARTMOOR PUBLIC TRANSPORT GUIDE

timetable booklet and ideas for countryside walks. Available from information centres or by calling (0626) 832093.

THE DARTMOOR VISITOR

Free newspaper gives details of guided walks & events in the National Park and is available from information centres or by calling (0626) 832093.

DARTMOOR WILDLIFE PARK, SPARKWELL;

58/59 from Plymouth. Daily. Admission Charge

DEVON BUS ENQUIRY:

(0392) 382800 or (0752) 382800 for timetable information on all bus services. (8.30am-5pm)

DEVON GUILD OF CRAFTSMEN,BOVEY TRACEY

Any bus to Bovey Tracey. Riverside Mill is in the the centre of the town.

DREWSTEIGNTON;

359 from Exeter. Daily. 671 from Whiddon Down. Less than daily. 174 from Okehampton. Summer service only.

DUNSFORD:

359 from Exeter & Moretonhampstead. Daily. 82 (Transmoor Link) from Plymouth & Exeter. Summer only.

ERMINGTON:

91 from Dartmouth. 608 from Ivybridge. Less than daily.

FINCH FOUNDRY STICKLEPATH

Any bus to Sticklepath. This National Trust property is in the centre of the village.

GREAT HALDON FOREST. NR EXETER

X38/X39 from Exeter and Plymouth to Haldon racecourse. Daily. 878 from Newton Abbot to Haldon Belvedere. Less than daily. Forest walks start in the main car park. Advisable to plan your route before visiting.

HATHERLEIGH;

A number of services from Okehampton throughout the week.

HAYTOR:

193 from Newton Abbot. less than daily. 170/171 from Newton Abbot. Summer service only.

HIGH MOORLAND VISITOR CENTRE, PRINCETOWN

Any bus to Princetown. The centre is in the middle of the village.

INFORMATION CENTRES

Ashburton, Main Car Park - personal callers only
Bovey Tracey, The Lower Car Park, Station Road
(0626) 832047
Ivybridge Leonards Road, Ivybridge
(0752) 897035
New Bridge Main Car Park
(0364) 3303
Newton Abbot, Bridge House, Kingsteignton Road
(0626) 67494
Okehampton 3 West St
(0837) 53020
Parke Barn Parke, Haytor Rd, Bovey Tracey
(0626) 832093
Postbridge Main Car Park
(0822) 88272
Princetown High Moorland View Visitor Centre,
Duchy Hotel
(0822) 890414
Steps Bridge, nr Dunsford
(0647) 52018
Tavistock Town Hall, Bedford Square,
(0822) 612938
Totnes The Plains (0803) 863168

IVYBRIDGE:

X80 from Plymouth, Totnes & Torquay. 88 from Plymouth. Daily.

LYDFORD GORGE, LYDFORD

118 from Okehampton & Tavistock. Daily. 86 from Barnstaple. Less than daily. See the Dartmoor Public Transport Guide for details of Sunday and Summer services.

MANATON:

671 from Whiddon Down. Less than daily. 171 Newton Abbot Circular. Summer service only.

MEADOWLANDS LEISURE POOL, TAVISTOCK

Any bus to Tavistock. Pool is alongside the River Tavy

MINIATURE PONY CENTRE, PRINCETOWN

82 Transmoor Link from Plymouth & Exeter. Summer only Admission charge.

MORETONHAMPSTEAD

73/173 from Newton Abbot. 359 from Exeter. Daily. 671 from Whiddon Down. Less than daily. 82 Transmoor Link from Plymouth & Exeter. 173 & 174 from Okehampton. Summer service only.

MORWELLHAM QUAY, NR TAVISTOCK

See the Dartmoor Public Transport Guide for details of Summer Sunday services. Admission charge.

MUSEUM OF DARTMOOR LIFE,OKEHAMPTON

Any bus to Okehampton. The Museum is adjacent to the information centre.

NATIONAL SHIRE HORSE CENTRE, YEALMPTON

93 from Plymouth & Kingsbridge. Daily. 91 from Dartmouth, X92 from Kingsbridge & Salcombe. Less than daily. (91,X92 stop on A379 near to the turning for the centre)

NORTH TAWTON:

628, 648 from Okehampton & Exeter. Less than daily

OKEHAMPTON:

118 from Tavistock, 227 from Launceston, 624 from Hatherleigh, 51,227,628,629 from Exeter. Daily. 86 from Barnstaple, 630 from Northlew, 633 from Halwill, 648 from Winkleigh, 670 from Crockernwell, 860 from Moretonhampstead, 900 from South Zeal. Less than daily. 174 from Moretonhampstead, 173 from Newton Abbot, 187 from Exeter, Tavistock & Gunnislake (rail connection from Plymouth). Summer service only.

OKEHAMPTON CASTLE:

Any bus to Okehampton then look out for Castle Road

ORCHID PARADISE, NR NEWTON ABBOT

72/73 from Newton Abbot. Daily. (ask the driver to stop as near to the entrance as is safe to do so.

PARKE RARE BREEDS FARM,BOVEY TRACEY

193 from Newton Abbot. Daily. 671 from Whiddon Down. Less than daily. 170/171 from Newton Abbot. Summer service. Also buses to Bovey Tracey and then walk approximately a quarter of a mile to Parke.

POSTBRIDGE:

98 from Tavistock & Princetown. Less than daily. 82 Transmoor Link from Plymouth & Exeter. Summer only.

PRINCETOWN:

98 from Tavistock. Less than daily. 82 Transmoor Link from Plymouth and Exeter, 170 from Newton Abbot & Tavistock. Summer only.

RAIL SERVICES

There are British Rail main line stations at Plymouth, Exeter, Newton Abbot and Totnes. Ring (0752) 221300 for information.

SHAUGH BRIDGE, NR BICKLEIGH

58/59 from Plymouth. Daily. The Plym Valley Cycle Way is accessible from here.

SOUTH DARTMOOR LEISURE CENTRE

Any bus to Ivybridge. The complex is next to the information centre.

SOUTH DEVON RAILWAY, BUCKFASTLEIGH

X80 from Plymouth & Torquay, 165 from Dartington, 164 from Kingsbridge, 89 from Dartmouth, 175 from Newton Abbot, 91, X93 from Dartmouth. Daily. There is also a BR mainline station in Totnes.

STEPS BRIDGE, NR DUNSFORD, STICKLEPATH

359 from Exeter and Moretonhampstead. Daily. 82 Transmoor Link from Exeter & Plymouth. Summer only 51, 629 from Exeter & Okehampton. Daily. 860 from Moretonhampstead, 900 from Okehampton. Less than daily. 174 from Okehampton, 187 from Exeter, Okehampton, Tavistock & Gunnislake. Summer only (Rail connection from Plymouth).

STOVER COUNTRY PARK, NR BOVEY TRACEY

X38/X39 from Exeter & Plymouth to Drumbridges roundabout then walk approximately a quarter of a mile on A382 towards Abbot. 72/73 from Newton Abbot. Daily.

TAMAR VALLEY LINE

Running between Plymouth & Gunnislake, the Tamar Valley line is an unforgettable journey. 14 miles of railway follows the course of the River Tamar. For more information on services throughout the year telephone British Rail on 0752 221300 or look out for the Tamar Valley Line leaflet in the Information Centre.

TAVISTOCK

98 from Princetown & Postbridge, 118 from Okehampton 83/84 from Plymouth, 185/615 from Bere Alston & Bere Ferrers, 622/623 from Calstock. Daily. 97 from Buckland Monachorum,621 from Lifton,86 from Barnstaple, 631 from Northlew. Less than daily. 170 from Newton Abbot, 187 from Exeter & Okehampton. Summer only.

TEIGN VALLEY GLASS & THE HOUSE OF MARBLES

X39 from Plymouth & Exeter, 72/73 from Newton Abbot. Daily. 170/171 from Newton Abbot. Summer only. All buses will stop at the roundabout on the A382 next to the House of Marbles if it is safe to do so.

THE WHEEL CRAFT CENTRE, CHUDLEIGH

Any bus to Chudleigh. The centre is at the bottom of Clifford Street.

WIDECOMBE-IN-THE-MOOR

193 from Newton Abbot. Daily. 170/171 from Newton Abbot. See Dartmoor Public Transport Guide for details of this and other summer services.

YARNER WOOD NR BOVEY TRACEY

National Nature Reserve. 671 from Whiddon Down. Less than daily. 171 from Newton Abbot. Summer only.

YELVERTON PAPER WEIGHT CENTRE

83/84 from Plymouth & Tavistock, 55 from Milton Combe, 118 from Okehampton. Daily. 48 from Plymouth, 86 from Barnstaple & Okehampton, 97 from Buckland Monachorum. Less than daily. 82 Transmoor Link from Plymouth & Exeter. Summer only.

SUGGESTED DARTMOOR READING

Dartmoor	*Worth*
Guide to Dartmoor	*William Crossing*
Industrial Archaeology of Dartmoor	*Helen Harris*
The King's England -Devon	*Arthur Mee*
Dartmoor Water	*William Crossing*
Dartmoor - A New Study	*Crispin Gill*
Invitation to Devon	*Joy David*
Dartmoor Granite & Its Uses	*Sheila Perigal*
Sun, Moon & Standing Stones	*J.E.Wood*
Megalithic Sites in Britain	*A. Thom*
Dartmoor's Mysterious Megaliths	*Brian Byng*
Dartmoor Legends Retold	*T.H. Gant & W.L. Copley*
More Dartmoor Legends & Customs	*T.H. Gant & W.L. Copley*
Dartmoor the Threatened Wilderness	*Brian Carter & Brian Skilton*

The Wide Blue Yonder Climbing Guide to Dartmoor
The Wide Blue Yonder Climbing Guide tothe Dewerstone
The Wide Blue Yonder Climbing Guide to Chudleigh, Torbryan, Ansteys Cove
Rock Climbs in the South West, South Devon and Dartmoor

MATRIX

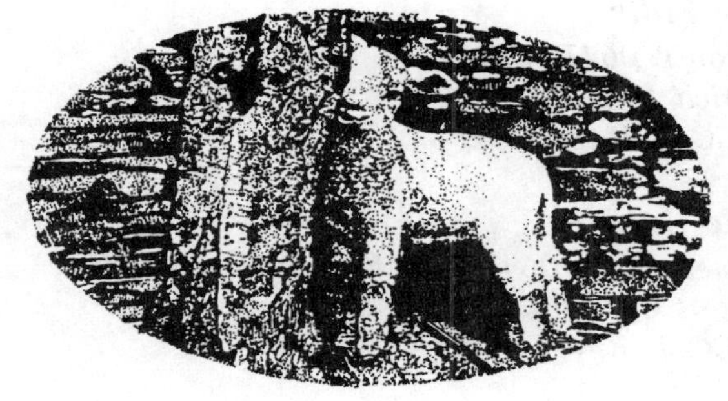

KEY

OH - Opening Hours
P - Parking
C - Children
CC - Credit Cards
L - Licensed
A - Accommodation
R - Restaurant
BF - Bar Food
V - Vegetarian
DA - Disabled
G - Garden
EC - Early Closing
LE - Live Entertainment
D - Deliveries

CHAPTER ONE

HOTELS - RESTAURANTS - INNS/PUBS

Anglers Rest

Fingle Bridge, Drewsteinton, T: 0647 21287
Apr/Sep 11/5.30 Oct/Mch 11/2.30 Mon/Sun, 7/11pm Sat
P, C, CC, L, A, R, BF, V, DA, G,

Castle Inn & Hotel

Lydford T: 0822 8242, F: 0822 82454
11/3 6/11 Mon/Sat, 12/3 7/10.30 Sun
P, C, CC, L, A, R, BF, V, DA, G

Drew Arms

Drewsteinton, T: 0647 21224

Lewtrenchard Manor Hotel

Lewdon, T: 0566 683256, F: 0566 683332
All Year
P, C over 8 yrs, CC, L, A, R, BF, V adv not, G

ATTRACTIONS

Becky Falls
Manaton T: 0647 722259
10/6 Mch/Nov
P, C, CC, L, R, V, DA, G

Castle Drogo
Drewsteinton, T: 0647 433306, F: 0647 433186
1 Apr/ 31 Oct Mon/Sun, closed Fri
P, C, CC, L, R, V, DA Ltd

SERVICE COMPANIES

Mountain Stream Activities
Wydemeet, T: 0364 3215
All Year
P, C

South Devon Hang Gliding Club
Poundsgate, T: 0364 3243

CHAPTER TWO

HOTELS - RESTAURANTS - INNS

The Anchor
Ugborough, T: 0752 892283, F: 0326 250350
11/3 5/11 Mon/Sat, 12/3 7/10.30 Sun
P, C, Cc, L, A, R, BF, V, DA Ltd

Bel Alp House Hotel
Haytor, T: 0364 661217, F: 0364 661292
Mch/Nov, Dec/Feb advance booking only
P, C, CC, L, A, R, V adv not, DA with asst, G

Brentor Inn
Brentor, T: 0822 810240 T
11/2.30 6/11 Mon/Sat, 12/3 7/10.30 Sun
P, C, L, A, R, BF, V, DA, G

Bull & Dragon Inn
Meeth, Doddiscombleigh, T & F: 0837 852939
Summer 11/5 6.15/11 Tue/Sat, 12/3 7/11 Tue/Sat, 12/3 7/11 Sun
P, CC,L, R, BF, V, DA, G

Burrator Inn
Dousland, T: 0822 853121/853370
11/11 Mon/Sat, 12/3 7/10.30 Sun
P, L, A, R, BF, LE

Cherrybrook Hotel
Two Bridges, Yelverton, T: 0822 88260
All Year
P, C, L, A, R, V, DA

Church House Inn
Nr Holme, T: 0364 3208
11/3 6.30/11 Mon/Sat, 12/3 7/10.30 Sun
P, C, CC, L, A, R, BF, V

Cleave Inn
Lustleigh, T: 0647 7223
Summer all day Mon/Sun, Winter 11/3 6/11 Mon/Sat, 12/3 7/10.30 Sun
P, C, CC, L, BF, V, DA, G

Cornwood Inn
Cornwood, T: 0752 837225
11/3 6/11 Mon/Sat, 12/3 7/10.30 Sun
P, C, L, R, BF, V, DA, G

Cridford Inn
Trusham, T: 0626 853694
11.30/2.30 6/11 Tue/Sat, 12/2.30 7/10.30 Sun
P, C, CC, L, A, R, BF, V, EC closed Mon

Dartmoor Inn
Merrivale Bridge, T; 0822 890340
11/3 6/11 Mon/Sat 12/3 7/10.30 Sun
P, C, CC, L, A, R, BF, V, DA, G

Drake Manor Inn
Nr Yelverton, T: 0822 853892
11.30/2.30 6.30/11 Mon/Thu, 11.30/3 6.20/11 Fri/Sat,
12/3 7/10.30 Sun
P, C, CC, L, R, BF, V, DA, G

East Dart Hotel
Postbridge, T: 0822 88213, F: 0822 88313
Summer 11/5 6/11 Mon/Sat, 12/3 7/10.30 Sun,
Winter 11/2.30 7/11 Mon/Sat Sun hrs
P, CC, L, A, R, BF, V, DA, G

Elephants Nest
Horndon, T: 0822 810273
11.30/2.30 6.30/11 Mon/Sat, 12/2.30 7/10.30 Sun
P, C, L, BF, V, DA, G, LE

George Hotel
Hatherleigh, T: 0837 810454, F: 0837 810901
11/3.30 6/11 Mon/Sat, 12/3 7/10.30 Sun
P, C, CC, L, A, R, BF, V, DA, G

Golden Inn
Highampton, T: 0409 231200
11.30/2.30 6.30/11 Mon/Sat, 12/3 7/10.30 Sun
P, C, L, BF, V, DA, G

Great Leigh Farm & Guest House
Doddiscombleigh, T & F: 0647 52058
All Year
P, CC, A, R, V by arrg

Half Moon Inn
Beaworth, T: 0409 23176, F: 0409 231673
11/2.30 6/11 Mon/Sat, 12/2.30 7/10.30 Sun
P, C, CC, L, A, R, BF, V

Harrowbeer County House Hotel
Yelverton, T: 0822 853302
Closed Xmas Day & New Year Day
P, C, CC, L, A, R, V, G

Highwayman
Sourton, T: 0837 86243
11/2 6/10.30 Mon/Sat, 12/2 7/10.30 Sun
P, L, A, BF Pasties Only, V, DA, G

Holne Chase Hotel
Holne, T: 0364 3471
All Year
P, C, CC, L, A, R, BF, V, DA, G

Horn of Plenty
Gulworthy, T & F: 0822 832528
12/2 7/9 Tue/Sun, Closed Mon
P, C, CC, L, A, R, V, DA, G

Ilsington Country House Hotel
Ilsington, T : 0364 661452, F: 0364 661307
All Year
P, C, CC, L, A, R, BF, V, DA, G

Jasmine Chinese Restaurant
Nr Yelverton, T: 0822 852807
6/11 Mon/Sat
P, C, CC, L, R, V Adv not, DA

Leaping Salmon
Horrabridge, T & F: 0822 852939
11/11 Mon/Sat, 12/3 7/10.30 Sun
P, C, L, R, BF, V, EC

Moorland Hall Hotel
Marytavy, T: 0822 810466
All Year
P, C, CC, L, A, R, V, DA, G

Moorland Links Hotel
Yelverton, T: 0822 852245, F: 0822 855004
11/2.30 6.30 Mon/Sat, 12/2 7/10.30 Sun
P, C, CC, L, A, R, BF, V, DA, G, EC

Nobody Inn
Doddiscombleigh, T: 0647 52394, F: 0647 52978
Summer 12/2.30 6/11 Mon/Sat,
Winter 12/2.30 7/11 Mon/Sat, 12/3 7/10.30 Sun
P, CC, L, A, R, BF, V, G

Oxenham Arms
South Zeal, T: 0837 840244, F: 0837 840791
11/2.30 6/11 Mon/Sat, 12/3 7/10.30 Sun
P, C, CC, L, A, R, BF, V, DA, G

Peter Tavy Inn
Peter Tavy, T: 0822 810348
11.30/3 6.30/11 Sat, 11.30/2.30 6.30/11 Mon/Fri,
12/3 7/10.30 Sun
P, C, CC, L, R, BF, V, DA with asst, G, LE

Rising Sun
Gunnislake, T: 0822 832201
11/3 5/11 Mon/Sat, 12/3 7/10.30 Sun
P, C, L, BF, V, G, LE

Rock Inn
Haytor Vale, T: 0364 661305, F: 0364 661242
From 7 am
P C, CC, L, A, R, V, DA, G

Rock Inn & Complex
Yelverton, T: 0822 852022
11/11 Mon/Sat, 12/3 7/10.30 Sun
P, C, CC, L, BF, V, DA, G

Royal Inn
Horsebridge, T: 0822 87214
12/2.30 Mon/Sun. 7/11 Mon/Sat 7/10.30 Sun
P, L, BF, V, DA, G

Royal Oak
Bridestowe, T: 0837 86214, F: 0837 86660
12/3 6.30/11 Mon/Sat, 12/3 7/10.30 Sun
P, C, CC, L, A, BF, V, DA, G, LE

Royal Oak

Dunsford, T & F: 0647 52256
12/2.30 7/11 Mon, 11.30/2.30 6.30/11 Tue/Thu, 11.30/3 6/11 Fri/Sat, 12/3 7/10.30 Sun
P, C, CC, L, A, R, BF, V, DA, G, LE

Royal Oak Inn

Meavy, T: 0822 852944
11/3 6/11 Mon/Fri, 11/11 Sat, 12/3 7/10.30 Sun
L, BF, V

Royal Standard

Mary Tavy, T: 0822 810289
11/3 6/11 Mon/Sat, 12/3 7/10.30 Sun
P, C, L, BF, V, DA with asst, G

Rugglestone Inn

Widecombe in the Moor, T & F: 0364 2327
11.30/2.30 6/11 Mon/Fri, 11/3 6/11 Sat, 12/3 7/10.30 Sun
P, L, BF, V, DA, G

Ship Inn

Ugborough T; 0752 892565
11.30/2.30 6/11 Mon/Sat, 12/3 7/10.30 Sun
P, L, R, BF, V, DA, G Patio, LE

White Hart

Bridestowe, T: 0837 86318, 11.30/2.30 7/11 Mon/Sat, 12/3 7/10.30 Sun
P, CC, L, A, R, BF, V, G

White Hart Inn

Chilsworthy, T: 0822 832307
12/3 6/11 Mon/Sat, 12/3 7/10.30 Sun
P, C, CC, L, A, R, BF, V, DA, G

Who'd Have Thought It

Milton Coombe, T: 0822 853313
11.30/2.30 6.30/11 Mon/Fri, 11.30/3 6.30/11 Sat, 12/3 7/10.30 Sun
P, L, BF, V, DA, G

ATTRACTIONS

Buckland Abbey

Buckland Monachorum, T: 0822 853607
10.30/4.45, Closed Thurs May/Sep, 12/5 wkends Oct/Apr
P

Finch Foundry

Sticklepath, T: 0837 840046
11/5 Mon/Sat Apr/Oct, Open Sun Jun/Sep
P, C, R Tea Room

Garden House

Buckland Monachorum, T: 0822 854769
10.30/5 Mon/Sun Mar/Oct
P, C, R Teas Lnch Apr/Sept

Morwhelham Quay

Tabistock, T: 0822 832766, F: 0822 833808
10/6.15 last entry 3.30 Easter/Oct, 10.30/4.30 Nov/Easter
P, C, CC, L, R Summer season only, BF, V, DA, G, LE Xmas Only

Paperweight Centre

Leg O Mutton Corner, T: 0822 854250
10/5 Mon/Sat Easter/Oct, 10/5 Sun May/Sep,
Winter 1/5 Wed 10/5 Sat
P, CC

Parke Rare Breed Farm

Cholderton, T: 0626 64438
10/4.45 Mon/Sun Easter/End Oct
P, C, R, DA, G

Roundhouse Craft Centre

Buckland in the Moor, T: 0364 653234
9.30/6 Mon/Sun Summer, 10/5 Mon/Sun Winter
P, C, CC, L, R, V, DA, G,

Rowden Gardens

Brentor, T: 0822 810275
Apr/Oct Sat/Sun, bank hols 10/5, or by appt
P, DA

SERVICE COMPANIES

Berrington Draughting & Technical Service
Bere Alston, T & F: 0822 840418
8/5 Mon/Fri
P

Countryman Cider
Felldownhead, T: 0822 87226
Summer 8.30/6.30 Mon/Sat, Winter 9.5.30 Mon/Sat
P, L Off Lic, DA

Crossways Riding School
Yelverton, T: 0822 853025
9.30/4.30 Mon/Sun
P, C. DA

Endsleigh Garden Centre
Milton Abbot, Tavistock, T: 0822 87235, F; 0822 87513
8/5 Mon/Sat, 2/5 Sun Feb/Nov
P, CC

Hugh Williams Accountant
Willsworthy, Peter Tavy, T: 0822 810286
9/5 Mon/Fri

Littlecombe Riding Centre
Holne, Ashburton, T: 0364 3260
Closed Mon & Wed
P, C

Longlands Field Study Centre
Hennock, T: 0626 833382
Feb/Nov
P A, V Ltd

Mill Leat Trout Farm & Craft Centre
Ermington T: 0548 830172
Summer 9/5.30 Mon/Sun, Winter Mon/Sat lunch time
P

Pixieland
Dartmeet, T: 0364 3412
9.45/6 1 Mar/21 Dec
P, CC, DA Garden only

St Mellion Hotel & Golf Course
St Mellion, T: 0579 50101, F: 0579 50116
All Year
P, C, CC, A, R, BF, V, DA, G

Tamar Fuels
South Brentor, T: 0822 86458
8/5.30 Mon/Fri, 8/1 Sat
EC Sat

CHAPTER THREE

HOTELS - RESTAURANTS - INNS/PUBS

Bedford Hotel
Tavistock, T: 0822 613221, F: 0822 618034
7/11 All year
P, C, CC, L, A, R, BF, V

Cornish Arms
Tavistock, T: 0822 612145, F: 0822 617196
11/2.30 5.30/11 Mon/Sat, 7/10.30 only Sun
P, C in rest, CC, L, R, BF, V, DA, G patio

Ordulph Arms
Tavistock, T: 0822 615048
11/2.30 5/11 Mon/Sat, 12/3 7/10.30 Sun
P, C in Rest, CC, L, R, BF, V, DA with asst.

Queen's Head
Tavistock, T: 0822 613048
All day Mon/Sat, 12/3.30 7/10.30 Sun
L, DA

ATTRACTIONS

Ambulance Museum
Tavistock, T & F: 0822 610066
From Sept 94 All year
P, C, CC, DA

SERVICE COMPANIES

Abbey Garden Marchinery
Tavistock, T: 0822 614053
8.30/5 Mon/Fri, 9/5 Sat
P, CC, DA, D

Dartmoor Photographic
Tavistock, T & F: 0822 614055
9/5.30 Mon/Fri
CC

Farleys Mens Wear
Tavistock, T: 0822 613559
9.30/5

G B Property Management
Tavistock, T: 0822 618104, F: 0822 61822

Hurdwick Golf Club
Tavistock, T: 0822 612746
8am to dusk Mon/Sun
P, L, BF, V

Kelly College, Tavistock
T: 0822 613005, F: 0822 616628

Kountry Kit
Tavistock, T: 0822 613089
9/5 Mon/Sat, 9/5.30 Fri
C

Lloyds House Bank
Tavistock, T: 0822 614567
9.30/4.30 Mon/Fri

Meadowland Leisure
Tavistock, T: 0822 617774, F: 0822 614321
7/10 Mon/Sat
P, C, CC, R, V, DA

Michael Taylor (Accountant)
Tavistock, T: 0822 614654 24hr Ans Mach
9/5.30 Mon/Fri or by appt.

N Creber Ltd
Tavistock, T: 0822 612266
9/5 Mon/Sat, 8.30/5 Fri
D free

Pillars News
Tavistock, T: 0822 612984, F: 0822 619311
6/5.30 Mon/Sat, 6/1 Sun
LE Sun

Sew-N-So
Tavistock, T: 0822 616621
9.30/5 Mon/Sat

Sunningdale Nursery
Tavistock, T: 0822 613416
8.30/4 Mon/Fri flexy

Tavistock Auction Rooms
Tavistock, T: 0822 610080
Every 2 weeks

Tavistock Golf Club
Tavistock, T: 0822 612049, F: 0822 612344
8.30/dusk Mon/Sat, 8/dusk Sun
P, L, R, BF, V adv not, DA

Tavistock Times
Tavistock, T: 0822 613666
8/dusk
P

Tavistock Trout Farm
Tavistock, T: 0822 615441
8/dusk Mon/Sun
P, DA

CHAPTER FOUR

HOTELS - RESTAURANTS - INNS/PUBS

Fountain Inn
Okehampton, T: 0837 53900
11/2.30 7/11 Mon/Sat, 12/3 7/10.30 Sun
P, CC, L, A, R, BF, V, DA, G

Heathfield House
Okehampton, T: 0837 54211
Feb/Nov
P, C, CC, L, A, R Dine Room, V, G

White Hart Hotel
Okehampton, T: 0837 52730
11/11 Mon/Sat, 12/3 7/10.30 Sun
P, C, CC, L, A, R, BF, V, DA

ATTRACTIONS

Museum of Dartmoor Life
Okehampton, T: 0837 52295
Easter/Oct 10/5 Mon/Sat, Jun/Sep 10/5 Sun
P, C, R Tea Room, V, DA Partial, G

Octagon Theatre
Okehampton, T: 0837 52001, F: 0837 55526
All Year
P, C

SERVICE COMPANIES

Okehampton Times
T: 0837 53640/1

CHAPTER FIVE

HOTELS - RESTAURANTS - INNS/PUBS

Gidleigh Park Hotel

Chagford
T: 0647 432225, F: 0647 432574
All year
P, C, CC, L, A, R, BF, V adv not, G

Globe Inn

Chagford, T; 0647 433485
11/3 7/11 Mon/Sat, 12/3 7/10.30 Sun
C, CC, L, A, BF, V, DA

Great Tree Hotel

Chagford, T: 0647 432491, F: 0647 432562
7.30 am/11pm Mon/Sun
P, CC, L, A, R, BF Ltd, V on req, DA with asst.

Ring o Bells

Chagford, T: 0647 432466
11/3 6/11 Mon/Sat, 12/3 7/10.30 Sun
P, C, CC, L, R, BF, V, DA, G

Sandy Park Inn

Chagford, T: 0647 432236
12/3 5/11 Mon/Sat, 12/3 7/10.30 Sun
CC, L, A, R eves, BF, V, DA

Three Crowns Hotel

Chagford, T: 0647 433444, F: 0647 433117
All Year
P, C, CC, L, A, R, BF, V, DA, G

Well Farm Guest House

Throwleigh, T: 0647 231294
All Year
P, C, A, R res only, V, DA

ATTRACTIONS

Cider Press Museum
Chagford, TL 0647 433474
10/5 Mon/Sun
P, DA

Stone Lane Gardens (Mythic)
Chagford, T: 0647 231311
May 30/Sep 25 2/6 Mon/Sun
P, C with adlt, DA Ltd, G

SERVICE COMPANIES

"Chagfords"
Chagford, T: 0647 432407
9/5 Mon/Sat
CC

Fowlers Estate Agents
Chagford, T & F: 0647 433595
9.15/5.30 Mon/Fri, 10/2.30 Sat

James Bowden & Son
Chagford, T: 0647 433271, F: 0647 433114
9/5.30 Mon/Sat
CC, DA

J Meredith Antiques
Chagford, T: 0647 433474
10/5 Mon/Sat
P, DA

Mariannes
Chagford, T: 0647 432233
9/5.30 Mon/Sat
EC

Whiddons Antiques & Tea Room
Chagford, T: 0647 433406
10.30/1 2/5.30 Mon/Sat
12/5.30 Sun

Willow Designs
Chagford, T: 0647 432565, F: 0647 432471
9.30/5 Mon/Sat
CC, EC Wed

CHAPTER SIX

HOTELS - RESTAURANTS - INNS/PUBS

Plume of Feathers
Princetown, T: 0822 890240
All Day Mon/Sat All Year, 12/3 7/10.30 Sun
P, C, CC, L, A, R, BF, V, DA, G

Prince of Wales Hotel
Princetown, T: 0822 890219, F: 0822 890575
11/3 6/11 Mon/Fri, 11/11 Sat, 12/3 7/10.30 Sun
P, CC Visa for food, L, R, BF, V

White Hart Hotel
Moretonhampstead, T: 0647 440406, F: 0647 440565
All Year
P, C, CC, L, A, R, BF, V, G

White Horse
Moretonhampstead, T: 0647 40242
11/11 Mon/Sat, 12/3 7/10.30 Sun
L, A, R, BF, V

ATTRACTIONS

Dartmoor Visitor Centre
Princetown, T: 0822 890414
10/5 Mon/Sun

Mearsdon Manor Gallery
Moretonhampstead, T & F: 0647 40483
10/5 Mon/Sat, pm Sun in Summer
CC

Miniature Pony Centre
Moretonhampstead, T: 0647 432400
10/4 Mon/Sun, closed Fri
P,C, CC, L, R, DA

CHAPTER SEVEN

HOTELS - RESTAURANTS - INNS/PUBS

Old Cottage Tea Shop
Bovey Tracey, T: 0626 833430
10/5.20 Mon/Fri, 10/2 Wed, 3/5.30 Sun
P, R, V, DA Ltd

Old Thatched Inn
Bovey Tracey , T: 0626 833421
11/3.30 6/11 Mon/Sat, 12/3 7/10.30 Sun
P, C, L, R, BF, V, DA with asst, G

Riverside Inn
Bovey Tracey, T: 0626 832293, F: 0626 833880
11/11 Mon/Sat, 12/3 7/10.30 Sun
P, C, CC, L, A, R, BF, V, DA not in room, G

ATTRACTIONS

House of Marbles & Old Pottery Restaurant
Bovey Tracey, T: 0626 835358
9/5 Daily
P, C, CC, L, R, V, DA, D mail order.

Riverside Mill
Bovey Tracey, T: 0626 852179
10/5.30 Daily
P, C, L Rest, R, V, DA gr floor

Ugbrook House
Chudleigh, T: 0626 852179
1/5.30 Jul/Aug, G Tours 2/3.45
P, C, DA

Whitstone Vineyards
Bovey Tracey, T: 0626 832280
8/12 noon Mon/Fri or by appt
P, CC

CHAPTER EIGHT

HOTELS - RESTAURANTS - INNS/PUBS

Golden Lion
Ashburton, T: 0364 652205, F: 0364 653293
11/11 summer, 11/3 7/11 winter, 12/3 7/10.30 Sun
P, C, L, A, R, BF, V, DA Ltd, G

London Inn
Ashburton, T: 0364 652478, F: 0364 653095
11/2.30 5.30/11 Mon/Fri, 11/3 5/30/11 Sat, 12/3 7/10.30 Sun
C, CC, L, A, BF, V, DA Ltd

Watermans Arms
Buckfastleigh, T: 0364 643200
11/11 Mon/Sat, 12/3 7/10.30 Sun
P, L, A, BF, V, DA

ATTRACTIONS

Butterfly Centre & Otter Sanctuary
Buckfastleigh, T: 0364 642916
10/5.30 Daily Mar/Nov
P

Pennywell South Devon Farm Centre
Buckfastleigh, TL 0364 642023
Easter/End Oct
P, C, R, V, DA

River Dart Country Park
Ashburton, TL 0364 652511, F: 0364 652020
Apr/Sep
P, CC, L, A caravan/camping, DA Ltd

South Devon Steam Railway
Buckfastleigh, T: 0364 643536
10/5.30Jun/Sep Mon/Sun, Apr/May/Oct Wed/Sun

READERS COMMENTS

Please use this page to tell us about PUBS, HOTELS, RESTAURANTS etc and PLACES OF INTEREST that have appealed to you especially.

We will pass on your approval where it is merited and equally report back to the venue any complaints. We hope the latter will be few and far between.

Please post to: Joy David, The Publishing House, and expect to receive a book or "T" Shirt as a token of our appreciation.

Name of Establishment:

Address:

Comments:

Your Name:..(Block Caps Please)

Address:..

....

AN INVITATION TO LUNCH, DINE, STAY AND VISIT

The following titles are currently available in this series:
To order tick as appropriate

Devon and Cornwall, Edition II	☐	£8.30 inc p&p
Somerset & Avon, Edition II	☐	£8.30 inc p&p
East Anglia	☐	£7.30 inc p&p
Mid-Shires	☐	£7.30 inc p&p
Heart of England	☐	£7.30 inc p&p
Wales	☐	£7.30 inc p&p
Southern England	☐	£8.30 inc p&p
North and East Yorkshire	☐	£8.30 inc p&p

To follow

Cathedral Cities of Southern England	☐	£12.20 inc p&p
Cathedral Cities of Northen England	☐	£12.20 inc p&p

Also by Joy David

An Invitation to Devon *(a very readable, gentle meander through Devon)*	☐	£7.30 inc p&p
An Invitation To Plymouth *(a contemporary, easily read book covering all aspects of the city)*	☐	£10.20 inc p&p

Name:...

Address:..

.... Tel:(daytime).......................................

Please make cheques payable to The Publishing House

The Publishing House, Fleet House,
15 Trafalgar Street, Plymouth, Devon PL4 9PE
Tel: 01752 256013 - Fax: 01752 250503

BECKY FALLS
A MUST
FOR ALL VISITORS
to
DARTMOOR
A PRIVATE ESTATE of 50
acres, set in a beautiful
deep wooded valley.
Good Safe Attended Car Park
Open 10.00am - 6.00pm
Easter to October
Becky Falls is on the B3344
Bovey Tracey to
Manaton Road
BECKY FALLS
DARTMOOR
K.T.J.
• Nature Trails • 70ft Waterfall
• Restaurant & Tea Rooms
• Ice Cream Parlour
• Excellent Craft-Gift Shop
• Picnic Areas • Toilets
'A Super Family Day Out'
For only £3.50 per Car ...
including all occupants!
NO OTHER ADMISSION CHARGES

For information on Dartmoor National Park and the work of the Authority please contact:-

High Moorland Visitor Centre
Old Duchy Hotel
Princetown
Yelverton
Devon
PL20 6QF
Tel. (0822) 890414

Send a large Stamped Addressed Envelope for the free annual newspaper:-

The Dartmoor Visitor

which gives details of where to go, what to see, riding, fishing, camping, guided walks, events and exhibitions.

There are eight Information Centres in and around the National Park. These are located at Princetown, Steps Bridge, Newbridge, Okehampton, Bovey Tracey, Postbridge, Tavistock and Ivybridge.

The High Moorland Visitor Centre, Princetown, is open all year round 10am - 5pm. The exciting displays here give a unique insight into the natural and cultural heritage of Dartmoor's high moorland. They cover wildlife, archaeology, geology, granite quarrying, peat working, mining, military training, water, farming, forestry, Dartmoor artists and writers and conservation.

NOTES

NOTES

NOTES

NOTES